The Gr

The Truth about Agenda 2021-2030, New Covid
Variants, Vaccines & Medical Apartheid

-

Mind Control – World Domination – Sterilization
Exposed!

Rebel Press Media

Disclaimer

Our other books

Check out our other books for other unreported news, exposed facts and debunked truths, and more.

Join the exclusive Rebel Press Media Circle!

You will get new updates about the unreported reality delivered in your inbox every Friday.

Sign up here today:

https://campsite.bio/rebelpressmedia

Introduction

Transhuman man to be integrated with global digital control system, 'Implantable 5G nanotech biosensor as early as 2021 in Covid-19 vaccines'

The Pentagon's technology development arm, DARPA, and the Bill & Melinda Gates Foundation are collaborating with the tech company Profusa in the development of an implantable nanotech biosensor made of hydrogel (substance similar to a soft contact lens). This biosensor, which is smaller than a grain of rice, can be injected along with a vaccine and is applied just under the skin, where it actually merges with your body. The nanotech component allows for remote monitoring of all information about yourself, your body and your health via 5G. The biosensor, which can also receive information and commands, is expected to be approved by the FDA in early 2021 - just in time for the planned global Covid-19 vaccination campaign.

DefenseOne wrote about this hydrogel biosensor back in March, which is "inserted under the skin with a hypodermic needle. Among other things, it contains a specially designed molecule that sends out a fluorescent signal once the body starts fighting an infection. The electronic part attached to (/in) the skin detects this signal, and then sends an alert to a doctor, a website, or a government agency. 'It's like a blood lab on the skin that can pick up, even before there are other symptoms like coughing, the body's response to illness.'

It is therefore not difficult to guess why this sensor may be considered of great importance by the elite in the (so-called) fight against Covid-19. Anyone who has this - irremovable - biosensor injected into their body will be quarantined by the government at the slightest infection, and may be subject to other coercive measures, even if the person in question is not sick at all, nor shows any symptoms of it.

Biosensor monitors all body functions and transmits them via 5G

By using hydrogel, the biosensor will not be seen by the body as an intruder and attacked, but rather integrate with it. Also, according to the company, the sensor can not only detect infections, but also monitor the oxygen and glucose levels in your blood, as well as your hormone levels, your heart rate, your breathing, your body temperature, your sex life, your emotions - in short, EVERYTHING. Through 5G, all this information can soon be transmitted to every medical and political authority.

Profusa is currently conducting a study with Imperial College, also funded by Bill Gates, which became infamous for its ridiculous predictions of doom regarding Covid-19, which soon turned out to be utterly bogus. However, it was based on these that the lockdowns, social distancing, and the associated partial destruction of the economy and the elimination of many civil liberties were made.

Transhuman humans to be integrated with global digital control system

The biosensor, which may therefore be incorporated into Covid-19 vaccines as early as 2021, comes very close to realizing the aspiration of a transhuman human, in which everyone is totally controllable and even steerable. The "new human," or the human 2.0 as envisioned by the tech elite around Bill Gates and Elon Musk, will be gradually transformed into a kind of cyborg between now and 2025-2030, and become an integral - and therefore irreversible - part of a global digital control system, in which personal freedoms will have completely disappeared, and even human free will, will have been taken away.

Not for nothing do we call this the system of "the Beast. For the first time in history, technology has advanced to the point where the biblical prophecies about the 'sign of the Beast' can be fully carried out and fulfilled.

This book is a compilation of our articles published earlier and new articles to expose the vaccines with the fitting context, regarding topics such as depopulation and world control by the globalist elite, if you would like to know more about subjects such as the great reset, we would advise you to read our other books too, and share them with everyone you hold dear.

We want to reach as many people as possible, that's why keep publishing our content, to make sure that if one title gets ignored, the other title still gets the attention, these subjects need.

If we want to win this war against humanity, we have to inform everyone about the reality of what is happening right now!

Table of Contents

Disclaimer.. 1

Our other books... 2

Introduction... 3

Table of Contents... 7

Chapter 1: Agenda 21 9

Chapter 2: mRNA madness 20

Chapter 3: Fake news propaganda 25

Chapter 4: Logistics of fear....................... 36

Chapter 5: Covid infertility? 40

Chapter 6: No more freedom 47

Chapter 7: No healthcare 49

Chapter 8: 5G agenda 53

Chapter 9: 5G nanotech biosensors 58

Chapter 10: Vaccine Passport Protests...... 61

Chapter 11: Protest = Terrorism? 63

Chapter 12: Killer jabs? 67

Chapter 13: Immune system suppression 73

Chapter 14: Passports & chips.................... 79

Chapter 15: Endless debt?........................... 84

Chapter 16: No more money? 92

Chapter 17: 1921-1922?............................ 100

Chapter 18: Hyperinflation 106

Chapter 19: Imminent depopulation 109

Chapter 20: Fuel shortage 116

Chapter 21: Food crisis 119

Chapter 22: The next world war? 127

Chapter 23: Pressure from the east? 135

Chapter 24: Berlin is a military target 138

Chapter 25: The West against Russia 141

Chapter 26: The new "Green Deal" 144

Our other books 147

Chapter 1: Agenda 21

'The nation state, freedom and your voice are being completely destroyed' - 'Only mass resistance can stop this anti-human agenda, which is already being implemented'

Café Weltschmerz has published an interview with a recognized top American expert regarding Agenda 21, which can be summarized as a power grab that will eventually place the entire world under one technocratic communist dictatorship, in which individuals and peoples will have no say at all, not even over their own health and lives. With the Covid-19 fear pandemic hoax, the next phase of this de facto coup against our freedom, democracy and right to self-determination has begun. Café Weltschmerz therefore doesn't put "The hidden agenda behind the destruction of our society" under it for nothing - a destruction that is also being deliberately carried out by world governments.

Independent journalist Spiro Kouras (Activist Post) interviewed the executive director of the Post Sustainability Institute, Rosa Koire, an expert on land use and property rights who has given speeches around the world. Her work can be found on the website Democrats United Against UN Agenda21, a website that was inaccessible at the time of writing.

Koire is also the author of the book "Behind the Green Mask - UN Agenda 21. Agenda 21 was signed by 178 countries and the Vatican in 1992. With this agenda, a globalist power elite wants to gain total control over all land, water, vegetation, minerals, construction, means of production, food and energy. Law enforcement, education, information, and the people themselves must also come under this complete control.

Agenda 2030: intermediate step in destruction of nation-state and freedom

Also, large sums of "money" must be moved from the developed to the less developed countries. Ultimately, it's about destroying your ability to have a voice, a representative government.' National governments turn into administrations. 'Your ability to be free and independent is being completely destroyed. The goal is to transfer power from local and individual persons to a global system of government... It is a plan to disrupt and destroy the existing system. It is a plan of transformation and control, and that is what we are experiencing now.'

Agenda 2030 is only an intermediate step in Agenda 21, just as 2020, 2025 and 2050 are. By 2050, with the help and support of big globalist names like Ford, Rockefeller, Soros, Gates, Zuckerberg, Musk, the Pope, and last but not least Rothschild, this perfidious plan must be completed. By 2050, all nation-states are to be abolished, and the world's population concentrated in a number of mega-cities that can encompass entire states and countries (just as the Netherlands, along with Belgium and the German Ruhr, is to become one big city).

'This is meant to crush your ability to control what happens to you. It is a global plan, but it is being implemented locally under different names.' This is done deliberately to divert people's attention from the real objectives.

10

Actually, everything called 'green' and 'sustainable development' falls under Agenda 21. This includes 'climate change', i.e., all climate accords and initiatives, and certainly Covid-19 . 'A global crisis requires a global response,' is their idea. 'And that warrants global governance.'

Climate change and the corona p(l)andemic 'are designed to send people into a panic, so bad that you literally fear you won't survive it.' Whether or not there really is such a thing as a climate crisis is not even relevant, according to Koire. It works so well, it would have been invented anyway (indeed, it IS invented, conceived, in the early 1990s, which is literally written in UN documents).

The 'Great (Green) Reset'

Skouras then points to the 'Great (Green) Reset' launched at the World Economic Forum in Davos. Koire responds that she 'does not want to be an alarmist' but is very concerned that this 'reset' is now being pushed through regardless of the cost to people and society. 'However, they are staying behind their Green Mask, because once that comes off, the soldier boots and trenches come out.' Literally. See also our December 4, 2019 article: 'UN can use military force against countries that refuse climate agenda' (/ 'UN can shove extreme measures down peoples' throats' - Madrid climate conference participants want tough deals on breaking down prosperity and freedom in Europe).

We have now reached the point where those in power hardly care about the objections and concerns of the people. 'That's a kind of message from them to us, that they no longer really care about us.' It seems that there is not much we can do about it anymore, but Koire believes that it is still possible.

Technology has now advanced to the point where two big goals, eternal life and being able to create life yourself, have come very close. 'These people have no ethical boundary, and that is very worrying. You saw this with the Nazis, with Stalin, and now. There is literally nothing to stop these people.'

Everything and everyone will be digitally connected

In the 'Fourth Industrial Revolution' that they have now set in motion, truly everything and everyone is to be digitally connected. 'They are talking about a new social contract. Well, with a contract, normally both parties have something to say about it. But this is a contract where none of us gets a say... This is one of the reasons why we see all this hysteria in the streets. This is because it's a lesson, a communication to us: this is what happens to you if you take to the streets and dare to stand up against our plan.'

'People ask me: who is doing this to us? That's your government. Your government has been taken over.' With the help of groups and movements such as Antifa and Black Lives Matter, an attempt is being made to spark an uprising. 'We are under attack.' This was the reason Koire turned his back on the Democratic Party. 'But parties are just a distraction. At the top, power knows no party. In this globalist takeover of power, all possible means are being used. The plan is to disrupt and disrupt, and that is what everyone is seeing now. This is the plan to destroy social cohesion, and that is very successful.'

She calls the situation now 'extremely dangerous' because this plan is supported by universities, foundations, companies and government agencies. 'All these parties have been indoctrinated, from kindergarten to university education. These are the 'agents of change' that have been activated.'

'Transformation' = demolition of the individual

The widely used magic word is 'transformation', of education, the economy, the police and society alike. 'Transformation is in reality about breaking down the individual, of your alliance to any 'old' system, such as your family, your 'old' thoughts, or your faith... It is a psychological technique that actually breaks down your personality, and then rebuilds it (according to their new standards).'

The term "institutional racism" also used by the European Government is "just an excuse to literally destroy your mind. Mao Zedong used it, Sung used it, and so did the Nazis. It is a technique by which your personality is broken down, in order to rebuild you as the new human being, the new world citizen.'

Human must merge with A.I.

In this process, A.I. (artificial intelligences) also comes into play. A (global) A.I. police force is coming, not made up of humans. Also, drones will at some point no longer be controlled by humans, but by A.I. 'I don't have to explain that then you get a really dangerous situation.' New Zealand recently officially launched its first A.I. police officer, and in

13

Singapore they are now using intelligent robots to enforce social distancing.

Skouras: 'This is essentially an anti-humanitarian agenda, where they want to merge human with machine (AI).'

By the Covid-19 measures, everyone has been declared a potential enemy of each other. The idea is that you no longer trust even your closest family members and friends. At the same time, our health is also being degraded, which Koire says is a very important part of the Agenda 21 plan. 'This is the plan to inventory and control everything, including your DNA (hence the government's insistence that as many people as possible get tested for Covid-19 - this will allow your DNA to be taken and stored immediately).'

With your 'social credit status' as in China and soon in the US and Europe, you have to 'prove' that you are a loyal and obedient citizen who is 'worthy' of continuing to live in the new order. The system, of course, has been doing this for some time now by favoring certain talented people, which the rest then have to pay for. The Chinese system is going to be rolled out across the planet.

Depopulation vaccine

'The Chinese also agreed in the 1990s to work with the US on a depopulation vaccine.' Did they go through with that? Is that vaccine now out there, and is it being 'sold' to humanity under a different name (perhaps a Covid-19 vaccine?)? Either way, 'depopulation is an essential part of the plan.' If it is determined that you don't have enough value, and/or are taking up too much space, using too much energy, too much water, too much land, then you must be 'isolated' and relocated.

The vast majority of humanity will be forced to live in ('multicultural') mega-cities, where every aspect of our lives will be controlled and managed 24/7/365. 'This plan will literally take all freedom away from you completely. And this is not about a plan for the future, but is something that is already happening right now. So, this is not just in 2030 or 2050. 2020 is really a very important year. A lot of these plans are now being rolled out at the regional level.'

'We have been massively misled by our leaders and their advisors,' said Dr. Mike Yeadon, former vice president at Pfizer, in an interview with Germany's Stiftung Corona Ausschuss just under two weeks ago. 'What I'm about to tell will shock everyone.' Yeadon warned that the constant 'topping up' of corona vaccines, as now seems to be the intention (the 'vaccine subscription' as we once called it last year) is not only totally unnecessary, but also life-threatening, because all these vaccines will not go through the normal approval process. 'Genetic sequences will be injected directly into the arms of hundreds of millions of people... This could cause serious injury and death in a significant proportion of the world's population.'

Immunologist and respiratory organs expert Yeadon - who, by the way, has been away from Pfizer for about 10 years - said he found the 'very large number of deaths' after the corona vaccinations 'no coincidence'. He called it "arrogant" of the vaccine manufacturers to assume that these new vaccines, which instruct the body to produce a spike protein of the corona virus, would not cause major problems,

15

because scientific studies had already shown the danger that this technology would cause a much too strong (auto-)immune response in very many people, which could make them seriously ill or even kill them. The past three months have shown that this is indeed the case.

'All these genetic vaccines (Pfizer-AstraZeneca-Moderna) represent a fundamental safety risk to the population,' he warned.

Because of the poor connection, Dr. Reiner Füllmich, one of the heads of the German committee, summarized what he had said. 'According to Dr. Yeadon, what is happening now is a very serious crime, committed by 'bad actors', our own political and self-proclaimed 'scientific' elite... The spike protein is biologically active, and is precisely replicated by the vaccines. This causes an autoimmune reaction, like a cytokine storm. Several thousand people have already died from this in Europe. In Israel, even 40 times as many people over 80 and 260 times as many younger people have already died from the vaccine than from Covid-19. From all other countries we get similar reports.'

'All vaccines stimulate your body to make that spike protein, and that's not a good thing for you... It's biologically active, initiates biological processes, and causes certain body functions to be totally disrupted or even destroyed,' Yeadon repeated.

Effects of vaccines can strike after days, weeks, months or even years

It depends on the immune system of the person and the reaction of his cells to the genetic instructions whether these effects occur immediately, in the short term, or only in the medium or long term. So, people who are vaccinated now and say 'nothing will happen' are definitely not safe. The effects can strike tomorrow, next month, next year, or even after a few years. If I were a (medical) institution I would no longer provide these vaccines,' Yeadon emphasized.

Meanwhile, tens of millions of Europeans and more than 100 million Americans have already been injected with them, and it doesn't look like politicians are even going to consider whether these "vaccines" packaged as genetic engineering are really as "safe" as the manufacturers claim.

Dr. Füllmich then reiterated Yeadon's words that the "vaccines" now being dispensed are in reality not vaccines, but "something completely different. It is only classified as a vaccine because it is used as a vaccine.' However, they are not vaccines, but substances that amount to gene therapy, to genetic manipulation. The worst thing is that a great many (serious) side effects may not be linked to these substances, precisely because they are falsely used as 'vaccines'.

'First step is awareness, second step: take action'

Can we still stop this? 'Awareness is the first step of resistance,' Koire says. 'Action is the second step.' People need to understand that we are now conditioned to remain passive, and to think that if we press 'like' on social media, we are politically active. 'But you're not a political activist if you don't leave your house.' Hence all these lockdowns and social distancing - they want to declare mass opposition to this Agenda 21 demolition and total control plan illegal and impossible in advance.

'And don't say that your government is so bad that there's nothing you can do about it. I'm sure it looks that way, but that's because you've let it get this far. It won't get any better if you just let this go on. That's why we think you really need to "occupy" your government (occupy, also "seize," "occupy," or "occupy"). BE your government. Yes, we are in the End Game, and there is not much time left. So, you should have done this a while ago.'

People need to start recognizing Agenda 21, even in their own locality and region. Bring it up in your local council. Continuously talk to representatives of the people about it. Probably every item on your city council's agenda is linked to Agenda 21.' She advises people to look at her website and read her book so that 'you're going to find out how they manipulate public opinion, so you're not going to cause problems for them. They want you to stay home in your chair.'

So, take action, speak to people and officials, hand out flyers, share videos, write and publish about it. 'Because just knowing that this is going on, without doing anything about it, is not enough anymore. You have to become politically active and be prepared not to immediately take over everything from them.' For example, they want to start replacing reality with VR (virtual reality), because it would make life so much more fun.'But as soon as you start doing that, your life is over. So, you have to resist.'

Don't believe Wikipedia, Agenda-21 is an anti-human agenda

18

'Wherever you work, wherever you are, talk about this.' Many people won't like that, and won't like you (anymore). But so be it, because this plan is real, and is being implemented right now, whether we like it or not. 'Agenda 21 is NOT what Wikipedia tells you. It is NOT voluntary, and not 'non-binding'. For you, this plan is mandatory.... So let's fight this together. We must all oppose it.'

They are selling it as something that will improve and save the world, the climate, the environment. But (Agenda 21 / 2030) is an anti-human agenda this is being implemented right now. We don't want to go down that dark path, this path to tyranny.'

Fake memorandum predicts permanent lockdown in a few weeks

A so-called British government memorandum would indicate that the country will go into permanent lockdown as early as 3 weeks or in August because - despite mass vaccinations - a 'third wave' with mainly the Indian Delta variant is expected. The document, whose authenticity cannot be confirmed and which is most likely fake*, is said to have been written by the infamous alarmist Dr. Neil M. Ferguson, who was discredited for his completely debunked pandemic models of last year, in which he predicted at least half a million deaths in Great Britain alone.

Chapter 2: mRNA madness

'This is a worldwide time bomb: ANY vaccinated individual will ultimately suffer detrimental effects, and autopsy on vaccinated persons confirms that mRNA and spike proteins move to all organs,' says an infectious disease specialist.

Several scientific investigations have decisively discredited the claim that Covid-19 vaccines only reside in muscle tissue, which has persisted for months. Now, an autopsy on a deceased vaccinated person would reveal that the genetic mRNA instructions, similar to the spike protein created by vaccines, propagated throughout the body to all organs. "This means that ultimately ANY vaccinated person will experience serious side effects," said a horrified infectious disease doctor from New Jersey who did not want to be identified for fear of retaliation.

Because this mRNA has converted vaccinated people into permanent "spike factories," the effects will almost certainly be irreversible. As a result, he concludes, "This is a worldwide time bomb."
The autopsy on a Covid-vaccinated man is reported to be the first of its type, revealing that 'viral RNA' was identified in practically all of the deceased 86-year-old man's organs 24 days after his injection.

When there is no Covid and a negative test, an ADE is triggered by a lethal vaccine-virus combination.

The man's health deteriorated after his first Pfizer shot on January 9, necessitating hospitalization after 18 days. He didn't have any clinical Covid symptoms, and his test came back negative as well.

As a result, "no morphological abnormalities related to Covid" were discovered in his body, according to the post-mortem report.

The 86-year-old caught Covid from another patient on the unit, according to medical authorities, but the autopsy shows that the damage to his organs occurred before he was admitted. That leaves just one possible cause: the vaccination. And when the man was infected in the hospital, he didn't stand a chance, suffering from an ADE reaction, which many independent scientists (including Professor Pierre Capel) and specialists have been warning about for months.

Vaccine mRNA produces virus RNA?

'The vaccine was unable to prevent the virus from infecting every organ,' explains Hal Turner, an American radio broadcaster. However, another possibility is that the 'viral RNA' was actually produced by the vaccine mRNA.

Finally, all vaccines approved in the West instruct the body to generate the virus's spike protein. Only this spike protein - purposefully engineered to better connect to human ACE2 receptors - is accountable for all health damage, according to a recent Pfizer study in Japan, and it spreads throughout the body after immunization, even to the brain, as shown in a recent Nature Neuroscience study.

In conclusion, the logical inference is as follows:

* if the body is bursting at the seams with 'viral RNA,' which would have killed the patient

* ... it has been demonstrated that just the spike protein is the virus's harmful component.

* and mRNA vaccines tell the human body to produce that spike protein.

* in a way that makes it stick to human cells even better than viral spike protein.

* The patient died as a result of an ADE brought on by the spike protein.

* He had no Covid-19 when he was admitted with health concerns 18 days after his vaccination, thus it must have come (primarily) from the vaccine.

People who continue to reassure others and themselves that they were "vaccinated months ago and have nothing to worry about" should remember that the repercussions of these intentional DNA modifications are similar to cancer in that they can develop swiftly but also slowly. Only one problem: once it's there, it won't go away on its own.

Are vaccines already having an impact on judgment?

We just wrote, 'Have nothing to worry about' Is it possible, however, for some persons who have been vaccinated to do so? I got a message from an acquaintance who said he had attempted everything he could to keep two of his pals from getting the vaccine. But it was in vain. Both pals were vaccinated notwithstanding; one is now continually racing, and the other had to be hospitalized due to serious thrombosis (anonymized info published with permission).

And, you guessed it, the doctors involved declared that it couldn't possibly be linked to the vaccine even before the diagnosis and examination. And, strangely enough, the victims believed it as well. Of course, this is all conjecture, but could this inability to think clearly, make sound decisions, and draw conclusions be the result of brain damage induced by those same vaccines?

'Time bomb on a global scale'

When he saw the postmortem report, an infectious disease specialist in New Jersey claimed he was stunned. 'People believe that only a small percentage of vaccine recipients experience side effects. Because these spike proteins attach to ACE2 receptors all across your body, this study suggests that everyone will ultimately experience negative effects.'

'That mRNA should have stayed where it was injected, but it didn't. As a result, the spike proteins produced by the mRNA will end up in every organ. And we know that the damage is caused by this spike protein.'

Chapter 3: Fake news propaganda

'How six months of Fake News absolutely affects you' - What is the 'logic' behind the PCR test and the allegedly increased incidence of 'infections'? : 'The earth is round, and so is a pancake. As a result, the world is a pancake' - The Oxford Covid vaccine was developed in human embryonic kidney cells that had been genetically engineered.

Professor (em.) of Immunology Pierre Capel starts his latest YouTube 'course' with the idea that' six months of Fake News can utterly transform you.' If you were asked a year ago if you would be genetically modified because you were terrified of getting the flu, what would you say? What do you believe your response was? But, after six months of Fake News, you've changed your mind and said, "Yes, please!" But do you know what viral genetic modification is? No, I have no idea, but 'it's our only hope, right?'

Capel also cites an official WHO bulletin from October 14, 2020, claiming that the IFR (mortality rate among the sick) for the entire population up to the age of 70 is only 0.05 percent, and corona is the same as seasonal flu, even among the elderly.

(Of course, the corporate media is spitting forth a new dose of terror today, proclaiming in big headlines that "between March and June, 168,000 more people died in the EU than projected." Simply look at the official

European statistics on EuroMOMO (especially the red dotted line with 'substantial increase') and you'll see that this is yet another deceptive, blatantly manipulative headline designed to keep you in a constant state of panic so that you don't think about what's really going on. It's not a big concern if there's a virus outbreak.

"We're going to talk about something that didn't exist, notably the second wave," Capel says. He refers to the official figures, which show that there were no more registered Covid patients at the end of June. Then folks went mad with PCR testing. Then you witness a massive outbreak of 'infections,' but is this really true? If this were true, there should be a significant increase in the number of persons who die. However, there isn't any.'

From a common pandemic to a bogus case outbreak

We had an epidemic that went on like the flu and passed until June; after June, we had a 'case epidemic,' which is an epidemic of purely positive PCR tests that, as you know, cannot show any virus, yield 94 percent false positives, and thus say nothing about whether someone is infected, let alone sick.

The image was the same in all countries: in the spring, we experienced "a typical seasonal viral respiratory infection," which happens every year. Covid-19 follows the same pattern as Covid-1 through 18. 'At the moment, there are very few hospital and ICU admissions, as well as very few deaths.' The PCR test is the sole way to identify the second wave.'

Then, in his trademark simple, accessible manner for anyone with a year or more of high school, he explains how a PCR test works technically. Essentially, the PCR test (by nose/throat swab) takes a small amount of RNA and exponentially amplifies it: after 35 rounds, 1 metaphorical molecule has been increased by half a billion times. Typically, one would end after 20 rounds.

The Second Wave of last year was made up entirely of useless and unproven 'infections.'

When you consider how many tests are now being performed at the same time, you can see how there is a creation of primers that cannot be lifted to make it fully pure. That's a big task, and it'll cost a lot of money.' The WHO wanted to know whether this is how you show a virus; it is NOT; you only show a small piece of virus - no infection, no live virus.

WHO decided that lengthy testing with three (suspected) virus primers was too expensive and time-consuming, therefore two primers were eliminated, and the third primer was only tested for 35 rounds. A PCR test normally has a multiplier of up to one million. But because there weren't enough positive tests, they increased the number to over half a billion! And if your primers aren't clean, well...'

To put it another way, there was no pandemic, but the government felt compelled to prepare for one regardless. And it was for this reason that the widespread use of PCR tests was set in motion.

First and foremost, the PCR test provides no information regarding the virus's viability. It's just a fragment of RNA that Might be from a virus, but could also be from a virus you had three years ago or something else else. That's where everything gets immunized,' says the narrator. He then displays the official WHO figures once more. The unfortunate reality is that this is Europe.

The number of 'infections,' as they call them, is represented by the blue line. So it's the PCR test that came back positive.' The green (hospitalizations) and red (deaths) lines, on the other hand, do not follow the blue line at all, and have remained largely unchanged for months.

The earth is round, a pancake is round; so the earth is a pancake'.

'Last year's Code Red and lockdown were predicated on the blue line, which just shows how many people were tested.' If we call it a second wave, that is! As a result, a "positive PCR test" has nothing to do with the concept of infection. It's similar to the following equation: 'The world is round, and so is a pancake.' As a result, the earth is a pancake.'

Yes, a few more people became ill with respiratory infections last year, but this happens every year (starting in the fall).

Excess mortality (from influenza, rhino, corona, RSV, and other diseases) was 7500 in 2016-2017, 9400 the following year, and 6130 in 2019-2020. We can now observe that the genuine'second wave' of 2020, based on genuine sick individuals rather than worthless PCR tests, is the first fall wave's typical sick people. What we are looking at in October 2020, is mainly the Rhino virus' (cold virusses).

For a (1.5) meter, social distancing, face masks, and lockdowns did not work.

According to international statistics, all "measures" (1.5 meters, face masks, and lockdowns) are ineffective for a single meter. We could spend hours displaying graphs demonstrating that the (official story) is incorrect. ' According to the media, Sweden, the class's naughty boy, took almost no measures, left everything open, and allowed society go on as usual.' And what do you think you're seeing? 'It's the same gradient,' says the narrator (with even a much lower peak as the countries with the strictest lockdowns, Italy, Great Britain and Spain).

Another clear example is the 47,600 popular pubs in the United Kingdom. It's quite impossible to keep a distance of 1.5 meters there; facemasks aren't used, and ventilation is frequently poor. With an average of 1,000 connections per bar every week, the total number of 'bad' contacts is staggering: 618,800,000 every week. What effect does this have on the number of sick and dead people? ZERO. There is no effect at all! If facemasks and 1.5 meters were truly effective, the number of sick and dead would have skyrocketed. Nothing, however, transpired.

After that, he displays a video of a test he conducted with numerous face masks. It is obvious that all versions worn by the general public are as porous as a sieve. There is no detectable effect in the statistics in nations that have made facemasks mandatory, such as Poland and Austria. As a result, facemasks are useless.

And what about the one-and-a-half meters? Nothing could be further from the truth.' For months, there has been a yes-or-no debate about whether large or little droplets are better (aerosols). Aerosols play a key role, according to a 2010 RIVM study. In that instance, you must maintain a distance of 10 meters rather than 1.5 meters. That makes no sense at all. Social distancing destroys the whole of society, but it doesn't make any difference to Covid.'

Measures are ineffective against viruses, but they are effective for fear.

Fog droplets are significantly larger than aerosols, yet do you observe them falling down within 1.5 meters when traveling through the forest? No! Aerosols float in the air. The importance of ventilation cannot be overstated. Outside, the issues are minor, and after the epidemic is ended, the difficulties inside are minor (but are related to ventilation).'

'As a result, we can tell that the virus's countermeasures are ineffective.' But what exactly do they do? On dread! On people's actions and social interactions. Everything is ruined!' In the less rich countries, it produces widespread poverty and other misery (mass unemployment, vast numbers of sick individuals). 'They are now dying like rats in nations like India and Indonesia. "But hey, as long as it's not here," Capel sarcastically adds.

'It's not a vaccine; SARS-CoV-2 protein is inserted into your genome'

'However, they've devised a solution: THE vaccination.' Things have already gotten out of hand a few times with studies like the Oxford vaccination (spinal cord inflammation / paralysis). 'Must be conceivable...,' Capel continues, sarcastically. ' But it isn't a vaccine in the least! It's genetic engineering. It's an adenovirus from a chimp that they've tweaked to allow it to infect humans. They cloned the spike protein (the protein that corona interacts to) into that virus. This isn't a vaccine; it's just genetic manipulation.' It was generated in human embryonic kidney cells that had been genetically engineered.

31

'How do they do it?' SARS-Cov-2 is a protein that may be inserted into your genome and expressed in a variety of organs. Then they merely wait for an immunological response to kick in and do anything. However, it has the potential to spiral out of control*. If we also see that human embryos are being utilized for this, and that some tumor genes are being inserted into them to make them develop, we can conclude that this is simply genetic alteration.'

(* What's our perspective on it? The next 'pandemic' will be caused by the Covid vaccine, which will be deployed in even more immunization rounds. The ultimate goal: every person on the planet must be vaccinated and so genetically changed on a regular basis, while the "refusers" must be ostracized and eventually eliminated away).

The entire human race will be genetically modified starting this year.

So, starting this year, the entire human population will be genetically modified on an unprecedentedly large scale over the world. Vaccination is a euphemism for this process. It's not a vaccine; it's a mixture of bacteria or virus proteins or membrane fragments mixed with a lot of garbage to stimulate the immune system. However, if you inject that into the body and it causes a reaction, it will go. The Oxford vaccine, on the other hand, is not a vaccine and will not disappear.'

Human embryos... HUMANS that have been genetically modified...

Because the coronavirus is prone to alterations, it's unclear whether these alterations are also present in the vaccine's spike protein. If that isn't the case (and the chances are quite high, if not near 100 percent), then this 'vaccine' is useless.

As a result, instead of vaccination, a new technology is employed: genetic alteration. There is a lot of misunderstanding about this. Animal testing is omitted with haste, and all sorts of things are yelled about, and this becomes the 'salvation' of everything. ' Capel depicts a dramatic image of an above-ground nuclear test in the 1950s in the United States, with hundreds of soldiers watching from a safe distance. They'd been advised that 'decent sunglasses' would be sufficient protection.. (By the 1970s, almost all of these guys had developed leukemia and other tumors).

Crowd control; mainstream media's monstrous misinformation campaign

'So the procedures are ineffective against the virus, but they are incredibly effective against crowd control.' Those measures are admirable, but for what purpose? It has nothing to do with the virus. In addition, there is a misinformation campaign going on (by the mainstream media, the OMT and the cabinet). We are constantly assaulted with bizarre stories, which makes us all very anxious, and we blindly follow all of the rules. These are having an effect, but on what do they have an effect?'

Control of the populace by a totalitarian regime

So, what are the benefits of lockdowns, 1.5 meters, and mouth caps? In order to maintain totalitarian control over the populace. Then you use all kinds of lies to terrify people. Then you induce massive hardship and misery via lockdowns, such as bankruptcies and famines.'

Then you use facemasks that make no sense at all to instill terror in people to the point where they ask for it. If you enhance people's terror, they will demand more dictatorship, as George Orwell predicted.

Big Pharma - Big Data - Big Banking - Big Reset - Big Scam!

Capel concludes, "I am not a conspiracy theorist." These measures, on the other hand, are prescribed internationally from a single source: the WHO, which is linked to other systems (including Bill Gates' GAVI vaccine partnership). One thing that is obvious is that this 'vaccine,' this genetic manipulation, is generating a significant amount of revenue... The government has previously spent a significant amount of money (hundreds of millions of dollars) on a vaccine that does not exist. This is a substantial sum of money for 'Big Pharma.'

'Then you realize that everyone is required to have an app, which may or may not be 'chipped.' Then there's 'Big Data,' the new gold, and 'Big Banking,' because money flows will be entirely altered (full payment digitalization in / from 2021).

So, how big of a 'Big Reset' and a 'Big Scam' is this? I have to say, this is incredible, and I could never have imagined it even in my wildest dreams.'

'There is a frenzied insistence on these tactics, which work really well for crowd control and societal destabilization, so now we are seeing emergency laws being passed that utterly eliminate democracy.'

Then, in March of the following year, elections will take place, right in the middle of Covid-20 (or Covid-21). Will they then claim that this is why they are unable to call an election?

Chapter 4: Logistics of fear

Dr. Hodkinson, the 20-year president of the biotech company that currently sells Covid-19 tests, cautions that the tests do not demonstrate clinical infection and blames "media and political hysteria."

More and more eminent scientists are speaking out against what is being done in the name of combating the current coronavirus, notably in the West. Dr. Roger Hodkinson, a virologist and pathology specialist, was the former chair of the Royal College of Physicians of Canada's Examination Committee of Pathology in Ottawa, the CEO of a large private medical lab in Edmonton, and the CEO and medical director of Western Medical Assessments, one of the producers of Covid-19 tests, for 20 years. Western's corona policy is "completely unjustified hysteria," according to Dr. Hodkinson, and "the worst scam ever perpetuated upon the naïve people."

Dr. Hodkinson remarked during a recent public video/audio meeting of an Edmonton City Council committee that Covid-19 is "nothing more than a go to flu season." This isn't the Ebola virus. It isn't SARS (-1). It's politics vs. medicine, and that's a hazardous game to play.'

'The simple truth is that the media and politics are fueling a completely baseless public frenzy.' It's ridiculous. This is the biggest ruse ever perpetrated on the general people.'

'Facemasks are absolutely pointless; no further policy is required.'

The scientist emphasized that no further measures are required beyond what is routinely done during a seasonal flu. 'When we were sick, we stayed at home and ate chicken soup instead of going to see Grandma.' We didn't need someone to tell us whether or not we should return to work.'

He claims that mouthguards are absolutely ineffective. 'There is no evidence that they work... (facemasks) are simply there to show that you are virtuous... You see all these people marching around like lemmings, obeying without question and covering their mouths with a mouthguard.'

'Everything needs to reopen tomorrow, and all testing has to halt.'

'At the same time, social separation is futile. Covid is dispersed via aerosols that travel 30 meters* before landing (*possibly 30 feet = roughly 10 meters). The unforeseen repercussions of lockdowns are horrifying! As stated in the (signed by tens of thousands of scientists, medics, and other specialists) Great Barrington Declaration, which I disseminated before to

this meeting, everything should be open again tomorrow.'

'I sell (Covid) tests, but I'd like to highlight with neon letters that positive test results do not imply clinical infection (as the media and politicians fraudulently claim with their statistics of 'infections')! Unless you submit yourself to the hospital with a respiratory ailment, (the tests) merely cause public frenzy and should be stopped...

All we should be doing is protecting the vulnerable and providing 3000 to 5000 I.E. of vitamin D to all nursing home patients every day, as this has been demonstrated to dramatically lower the (risk of) infection.'

'What is being done now is utterly ludicrous.'

'I remind you that according to Alberta's own data, the probability of death for persons under 65 is one in 300,000.' You guys need to get a handle on this. Given the ramifications, the scale of your reaction, which you are undertaking without any evidence, is completely ludicrous. Suicides, company closures, funerals, weddings, and other events abound. It's ridiculous, because it's nothing more than a terrible flu.'

'Let people make their own choice,' Hodkinson concluded, advising governments. You should be completely deafeningly deafeningly deafeningly deafening The provincial director of public health is deceiving you. I'm outraged that it's gotten to this point. It should all come to an end tomorrow.

Chapter 5: Covid infertility?

Based on these official documents, women who wish to have children should think twice about being vaccinated against Covid-19 -British Government Committee on Vaccination and Immunization: "Pregnancy should be ruled out before vaccinating, and we have not studied interactions with other medication"

The leaflets and care instructions for the Pfizer/BioNTech 'nano' mRNA vaccine, which will be administered to the UK population from next week, explicitly warn not to give the vaccine to children under 16 and pregnant women: 'Before vaccinating, pregnancy should be excluded.' People with weakened defenses-who have not participated in the clinical trial phases-and those who take medications regularly are 'advised' to contact a doctor first. Women who have the vaccine injected should take care not to become pregnant for the first 2 months after the second dose, which must be taken 21 days after the first.

You may be saying: these warnings aren't that abnormal, are they? They are also found in most package inserts of regular medicines. Indeed, they are. However, these are drugs intended for people suffering from a disease or condition, not for healthy people, all of whom should now receive a Covid vaccine.

The Joint Committee on Vaccination and Immunization has advised pregnant women and women who want to become pregnant not to take the vaccine at all. This means that the vaccine is simply not considered safe for these groups.

'No interaction studies with other medicinal products'

Caregivers are given the special warning in these instructions that medics and equipment should be kept ready "in case of a rare anaphylactic event following administration of the vaccine. We recently reported that official documents show that the British government, however, expects "a high number" of serious adverse reactions, so-called A.D.R.'s (Adverse Drug Reactions). A.D.R.'s include serious illness, long-term or permanent illness and disability, and deaths.

'As with any vaccine, vaccination with Covid-19 mRNA vaccine BNT162b2 does not protect all vaccine recipients. No data are available on the use of this vaccine in persons who have previously received a full or partial series with another Covid-19 vaccine.' In addition, 'no interaction studies (with other medicinal products) have been conducted.' It will be clear why we underlined this, because in Germany alone, millions of people take one or more medications every day.

There are quite a few over-16s who experienced 'mild to moderate' side effects during the test phases: 80+% had pain at the site of vaccination, 60+% experienced fatigue, 50+% headaches, 30+% muscle aches, 30+% chills, 20+% joint pain, and 10+% fever. These side effects "usually went away a few days after vaccination. Redness and swelling of the injection site and nausea were also among the "frequent" side effects.

No testing with people with weakened immune system

People with demonstrably weakened immune systems were excluded from the clinical trial phases. In the second phase, although 40% of the test subjects were people over 56, the statistics actually show that Covid-19 poses hardly any danger to people up to 70 (WHO confirmed IFR of only 0.05%). Have people over 70 been tested at all? Presumably not, as most of them have weakened or even non-functioning immune systems.

In fact, the UK government itself is not even sure the vaccine will work: 'The vaccine elicits both neutralizing antibodies and a cellular immune response to the spike (S) antigen, which may help protect against Covid-19 disease.' (bold and underlined added). This alone cancels out the average 95% efficacy during the clinical trial phases also reported in these instructions. That percentage is also based on the PCR test, now totally debunked for this purpose, which was used to test participants in both the vaccinated group and the placebo group to see if they had become 'infected'.

Unknown what the effects are on human fertility and development

But it doesn't stop here. The instructions to health care providers literally state that "it is unknown whether the Covid-19 mRNA vaccine BNT162b2 affects fertility. So that means that there is a chance that this vaccine may make you infertile.

At 4.6 'Fertility, pregnancy and lactation' it is stated that 'there is no, or a limited amount of data from the use of Covid-19 mRNA vaccine. Animal reproductive toxicity studies have not been completed. Covid-19 mRNA vaccine BNT162b2 is not recommended during pregnancy. For women of childbearing age, pregnancy should be excluded before vaccination. In addition, women who may give birth to children should be advised to avoid pregnancy for at least 2 months after their second dose.'

Under section 5.3 'Preclinical safety data' it is reaffirmed that 'Non-clinical data show no special hazard for humans based on a conventional study with repeated doses of toxicity. Animal studies of potential toxicity to reproduction and development have not been completed.' (emphasis added)

Let this sink in for a moment.

The animal trials to see if this vaccine has any effects on reproduction, i.e. reproduction, and development, have not even been completed. This means that we have no idea (yet?) whether this vaccine will affect the reproduction and development of anyone who receives

43

it. Or perhaps they do have an idea, and were so shocked by the results that they decided not to even complete the tests on animals?

Alleged GSK whistleblower: 'Vaccine caused 97% sterility in test phase'

On November 21, we wrote in our article "Nano particles in Pfizer vaccine according to minister De Jonge 'risk', but vaccine will be there anyway": American presenter David Knight recently cited a whistleblower from pharma giant GSK (link works again), who revealed that so-called 'anti-HCG' (hormone) adjuvants in corona vaccines cause 97% sterility. Indeed, during a clinical trial of the GSK vaccine, 61 out of 63 women were reported to have become infertile.

In a variant developed for men with an anti-GNRH (hormone), the testes would shrink, testosterone levels would drop, and the mitochondrial DNA in sperm would be destroyed, causing infertility in women. This was allegedly observed during vaccine tests on baboons.

According to the British spokesman for Govote.org, which Knight showed a video clip of, this will result in masses of people dying from Covid-19 vaccines in the coming years, while virtually no more children will be born. 'If this is their intention, we will have a massive global population reduction, which Bill Gates has been talking about for years.' That's why Govote.org wants the vaccines tested in independent laboratories.

'Vaccine can attack essential protein in women making them infertile'

The mRNA vaccines are going to program the body itself to make antibodies against the 'spike' protein of the SARS-CoV-2 virus. The now following unconfirmed information about this needs further study and verification: 'Spike proteins also contain syncytin homologous protien, which are essential for the formation of the placenta in mammals such as humans. It should be absolutely ruled out that a vaccine against SARS-CoV-2 can trigger an immune response against syncytin-1, because otherwise infertility of indefinite duration may occur in vaccinated women.'

'The vaccine contains a spike protein called syncytin-1, vital for the formation of human placenta in women. If it (vaccine) works and we thus form an immune response against the spike protein, we are also training the female body to attack syncytin-1, which can lead to infertility in women.

Since these vaccines are forced on us, but nevertheless you are given full responsibility in advance if things go wrong, this therefore means that IF you as a woman or man do indeed become infertile because of this vaccine, you are entirely to blame. After all, the manufacturers and medical authorities are already not holding themselves liable for this. Nevertheless, you will soon be punished if you refuse these vaccinations, and you may be denied access to airplanes, buildings, stores and events. And that will probably only be the beginning of the total social and societal exclusion.

Chapter 6: No more freedom

The US federal Occupational Safety and Health Administration (OSHA) is warning employers that they will be held liable for any damage to their employees' health if they are required to be vaccinated against Covid-19. This could become a tricky issue in Europe as well, since the government has rejected all government liability in advance and put it on the plate of health care providers. If in the end no agency wants to take responsibility, then in view of human rights these vaccinations cannot possibly be directly or indirectly made a condition for getting or having a job, or access to buildings and events, as is now the intention.

If a U.S. worker is forced to be injected with these experimental mRNA gene therapies packaged as "vaccines" and is subsequently blinded or paralyzed, or even dies, this injury will be considered "work related," which will make his employer liable. The guidelines also state that employers are required to record (serious) side effects and adverse reactions following Covid vaccinations in their employees.

The new OSHA directive was published on April 20, and was a response to companies and institutions that had announced that all their employees will be required to be vaccinated, such as the Methodist Hospital network in Houston. Those who refuse will first be suspended, and later fired.

Vaccines only have emergency authorization

It is expected that this hospital organization and many other employers will be sued if they follow through with these plans and their employees subsequently become ill or die. According to the VAERS registration system, nearly 200,000 Americans have already suffered health damage from the Covid-19 vaccines, and nearly 4,000 have died. Nearly 20,000 have been seriously (long-term or permanent) injured (autoimmune diseases, paralysis, blindness, the muscle disease ALS, Creutzfeld-Jakob, Alzheimer's, etc.).

America's Frontline Doctors (AFLDS) warns that the vaccines - as in Europe - have only a temporary emergency license, and for that reason alone cannot be imposed on anyone. 'The US Food & Drug Administration's emergency authorization specifically states that individuals should have the free choice to accept or refuse these vaccines,' LifeSiteNews explained. 'Many point out that any dismissal for refusing vaccines absolutely undermines your necessary freedom.'

However, the European Human Rights Court recently ruled that mandatory vaccinations are legal. Still, even in the Netherlands, not one worker should automatically accept that his boss requires a Covid-19 vaccination as a condition for keeping your job, or continuing to do the work for which you were hired.

Chapter 7: No healthcare

Some doctors are so indoctrinated and terrified that they blame the sick themselves: 'My employer put a lot of pressure on me to be vaccinated.'

The Highwire, the fastest growing American Internet health program that already has more than 75 million viewers, recently focused attention on a troubling trend in the U.S. that may also be occurring in other Western countries. In fact, more and more doctors are refusing to treat people who suffer from serious side effects and adverse reactions after vaccination with a Covid-19 vaccine. The reason is obvious: the political and pharmaceutical establishment has effectively canonized these gene-manipulated vaccines. If people do get very sick or even die from them - in the U.S. in 2021 there will already be 4000% more vaccine victims than in the whole of 2020 from all other vaccinations combined - then the instructions are that it cannot and must not be the vaccine's fault. Doctors who nevertheless observe this must fear for their jobs and careers.

Some doctors are so indoctrinated that they blame the sick themselves. They call people who suffer serious side effects after vaccination patients with a 'conversion disorder', afraid to put in their file that the vaccine is the probable cause. (Or, in other words, 'go back home, little lady, because it's between your ears.')

'On January 4, I was put under great pressure by my employer to get vaccinated,' Shawn Skelton told me. After she complied, she immediately experienced side effects such as mild flu-like symptoms. 'But by the end of the day, my legs were hurting so badly that I couldn't take it anymore. When I woke up the next day my tongue was twitching, and then it got worse and worse. The next day I had convulsions all over my body. That lasted 13 days.'

'Too afraid to treat us,' they say.

'One doctor told me the diagnosis was, 'I don't know what's wrong with you, therefore we blame you,'" said another. Skelton elaborated. 'Doctors just do not know how to address the mRNA vaccine's negative effects. I also believe they are terrified of it. I'm at a loss for words as to why no doctor wants to help us.'

Two other healthcare workers, Angelia Desselle and Kristi Simmonds had similar experiences. They too suffered convulsions, and their doctors also refused to treat them. A neurologist rejected Desselle's email referral to him. 'He was a movement disorder specialist, which I thought I needed. My primary care physician said it looked like I had advanced Parkinson's. But he emailed back that he had very complex duties, and he couldn't see me at that time.'

As other doctors likewise kept the door closed to her, she went to a neurologist without mentioning that she

50

had been vaccinated against Covid-19. 'I didn't want to be sent away again. But it is in my medical record, so when he looked at that he said 'so you took the vaccine?' And I said 'yes, but I didn't want to give you that information because I need help.' Now she is finally receiving treatment for her migraine attacks.

In Europe, general practitioners and specialists are subject to stringent regulations.

We don't know if general practitioners in Europe also refuse to treat vaccinated patients who become unwell. They are, however, prohibited from prescribing proven-effective and safe drugs to (suspected) corona patients, such as hydroxychloroquine and Ivermectin. Nothing should threaten the "holy" mass vaccination program - recovery: genetic engineering program, after all.

In Europe, general practitioners and specialists are subject to stringent regulations.

We don't know if general practitioners in Europe also refuse to treat vaccinated patients who become unwell. They are, however, prohibited from prescribing proven-effective and safe drugs to (suspected) corona patients, such as hydroxychloroquine and Ivermectin. Nothing should threaten the "holy" mass vaccination program - recovery: genetic engineering program, after all.

Earlier this year, the government put any responsibility for the consequences of the Covid vaccinations on the shoulders of health care providers and the people who are vaccinated with them. It is therefore not inconceivable that healthcare professionals and specialists in Europe will be reluctant to recognize, let alone treat, vaccination victims as such.

Chapter 8: 5G agenda

Governments want to push 5G through because it allows citizens to be tracked and monitored 24/7/365

The number of scientists who have major reservations about the introduction of 5G is steadily growing. The British epidemiologist Professor John William Frank of the University of Edinburgh is calling for the rollout of 5G worldwide to be suspended for the time being, until it has been independently confirmed and proven that the technology is safe and poses no danger to health Until now, governments have relied almost exclusively on studies by (or sponsored by) the big Tech companies, and of course they will never put their billion-dollar profits at risk by rejecting their own products.

Professor Frank is not against 5G, but he does think that far too little research has been done on it. That's why he argues that it's better to err on the side of caution, and freeze the rollout of the new mobile data traffic systems for now.

There are a lot more antennae and a lot more EMF radiation.

Frank, like many other academics, writes in the Journal of Epidemiology & Community Health that the primary threat of 5G is the massive antenna density required for these extremely high frequencies. Every few lampposts, a new antenna must be placed, exposing people to even more electromagnetic radiation (EMF). A federal commission of specialists in the United States has acknowledged the health harm that existing networks such as 4G and WiFi can cause.

Despite this, almost no credible epidemiological research on the impact of 5G on human health have been undertaken, according to the professor. Furthermore, 5G employs not just considerably higher frequencies, but also an entirely new supporting technology to handle massive volumes of data. For 5G to work, billions of antennas and signal amplifiers must be put every 100 to 300 meters around the planet. Amazon's upcoming 3,236 5G satellites, as well as the 12,000 to 30,000 Elon Musk plans to deploy into orbit, will soon cover areas where antennas are not conceivable.

'A rising number of worldwide engineers, scientists, and doctors are urging countries to raise their RF-EMF safety standards, commission more and better research, and halt further public exposure increases until there is stronger evidence that it is safe.'

The precautionary principle dictates that 5G deployment be halted.

Professor Frank isn't convinced that 5G and other EMFs are damaging to health and the environment, despite the fact that the WHO and a slew of tech experts assert otherwise. He believes that the spread of 5G should be halted immediately due to the "precautionary principle." You should not take any unnecessary chances when it comes to human health. That premise should be sufficient grounds to 'declare a ban on that (5G) exposure, pending adequate scientific inquiry into the alleged health risks.'

He goes on to explain that there is no compelling need to roll out 5G at a rapid speed in terms of public health and safety. It is being done primarily because the new technology will provide a significant boost to the Big Tech industry. With the existing 4G network, consumers have no shortage of rapid mobile data connections.

Governments want 5G to be implemented as soon as possible in order to have complete global control.

Frank neglects to add that governments are just as invested in 5G as the tech and media behemoths. The Bill & Melinda Gates Foundation and the Pentagon's technology development arm, DARPA, have teamed up with the tech firm Profusa to develop an implantable nanotech biosensor made of hydrogel (a substance similar to a soft contact lens) that can be injected alongside a vaccine and applied just beneath the skin, where it actually merges with your body. All information about yourself, your body, and your health may be controlled remotely thanks to the nanotech component.

As a result, 5G enables a global totalitarian control system that dictatorships of the past could only dream of. It will allow anyone's location, movements, and actions - and, in the not-too-distant future, thoughts and emotions - to be tracked, monitored, and manipulated 24 hours a day, seven days a week, while all personal information, such as vaccination status and bank balances, will be instantly accessible. Countless surveillance cameras with facial recognition and social-credit status checks are linked to this system, as is the Microsoft system (with patent no. 2020-060606) that converts your own body into a means of payment (and ID/vaccination proof) that is already in the testing phase.

According to some, a distance of at least one and a half meters is required for this system to function correctly, because signals can be disrupted if bodies are too close together.

It's unclear whether this is true, but without social distancing, surveillance cameras (and even smartphones) will have a much harder time scanning all foreheads in a crowded crowd in real time for the presence of the fluorescent M-Neongreen / Luciferase enzyme, the injected mark that in the future could serve as proof that you've been properly vaccinated and thus have access to society.

Is there a conspiracy theory?

Given that multiple scientists and other professionals have stated for months that 1.5 meters makes no difference in the alleged transmission of a virus, it's past time for more people to wonder why "social separation" must continue to be enforced unabatedly. Unfortunately, certain odd conspiracy theories, such as that 5G would trigger the coronavirus, and terrible deeds, such as setting fire to transmission towers, have polluted real concerns to 5G (intentionally?).

Politicians, the tech industry, and all mainstream media and magazines that rely on one another in any way invariably claim that these are all debunked "conspiracy theories," but when even the venerable Scientific American published an article on October 17, 2019, with the headline "We have no reason to believe that 5G is safe - Contrary to what some people say, there may be health risks,"

*'Implantable 5G nanotech biosensor as early as 2021 in
Covid-19 vaccines' Humanity evolving into transhuman
in future is integrated with global digital control system.*

DARPA, the Pentagon's technology development arm,
and the Bill and Melinda Gates Foundation are working
with Profusa to develop an implanted nanotech
biosensor constructed of hydrogel (substance similar to
a soft contact lens). This biosensor, which is about the
size of a grain of rice, is injected with a vaccine and
placed just beneath the skin, where it blends in with
your body. Through 5G, the nanotech component
enables remote monitoring of all information about
yourself, your body, and your health.

The FDA is likely to approve the biosensor, which can
also receive information and commands, in early 2021,
just in time for the planned global Covid-19 vaccine
campaign.

In March, DefenseOne reported on a hydrogel
biosensor that is "inserted underneath the skin with a
hypodermic needle." It contains, among other things, a
specifically engineered molecule that emits a
fluorescent signal once the body begins to fight an
infection. This signal is detected by the electronic
component attached to (/in) the skin, which
subsequently transmits a warning to a doctor, a
website, or a government agency. 'It's basically a skin-

based blood lab that can detect the body's response to disease even before other signs like coughing appear.'

All physiological processes are monitored by biosensors and transmitted over 5G.

The biosensor will not be perceived as an intruder by the body and attacked as a result of its use of hydrogel, but will instead integrate with it. The sensor can also track your hormone levels, heart rate, respiration, body temperature, sex life, emotions, and anything else, according to the manufacturer. All of this data will soon be delivered to every medical and government authority via 5G.

Profusa is now working on a study with Imperial College, which was made famous by its ludicrous forecasts of doom over Covid-19, which were quickly proven to be completely false. Lockdowns, social isolation, and the related partial collapse of the economy, as well as the removal of many civil liberties, were all founded on these.

Transhuman human being is integrated with global digital control system

The biosensor, which may therefore be incorporated into Covid-19 vaccines as early as 2021, comes very close to realizing the aspiration of a transhuman human, in which everyone is totally controllable and even steerable. The 'new human', or the human 2.0 as envisioned by the tech elite around Bill Gates and Elon Musk, will be gradually transformed into a kind of cyborg between now and 2025-2030, and become an integral - and therefore irreversible - part of a global digital control system, in which personal freedoms will have completely disappeared, and even human free will will will have been taken away.

Chapter 10: Vaccine Passport Protests

More than 70 parliamentarians rally against this 'heinous trap'

In an open letter to Prime Minister Boris Johnson, more than 1,200 British Christian leaders asked him not to adopt testing and vaccination passports.

In fact, they label it "the most dangerous proposition ever" since it amounts to "an unethical form of pressure" to force people to be Covid-19 tested or vaccinated.

Various denominations, including Anglican and Catholic, have leaders in the church. They believe that test and vaccine passports are the precursor to a "surveillance state," a totalitarian control state, and that they will put an end to what is left of liberal democracy.

The government in London maintains that no final decision has been reached, but all indicators point to these test/vaccination passports arriving soon, just as they did in Europe.

They will initially be marketed as a passport to more 'freedom' (catering, events, shopping, etc.), but as they become more prevalent, the standards will become increasingly strict, eventually eliminating untested and unvaccinated people from society entirely.

'Medical Apartheid' is a term used to describe a system of medical discrimination.

According to church leaders, such passports result in "medical apartheid... It establishes a surveillance state in which the government controls certain parts of citizens' life through technology. Over the course of a few years, that 'certain' threatens to be expanded to ALL areas.

'This is one of the most hazardous policy ideas ever made in the history of British politics,' warn church leaders, who emphasise that they will never deny those without such a passport access to their churches, regardless of the government's decision.

'Discrimination' and 'horrific trap' are two words that come to mind.

More than 70 British legislators openly protested the planned test/vaccination passports earlier this month. They claim that needing to show such proof in order to enter a pub, for example, is discriminatory. It also creates further societal divisions. (In any case, the West's entire approach is based on 'divide and rule.')

Conservative MP Steve Baker even termed these passports "a nasty trap." Labour leader Sir Keir Starmer expressed "great alarm" over this looming new form of discrimination.

Chapter 11: Protest = Terrorism?

No one wants to hear it, no one is allowed to say it, but everyone knows where this could end up.

While Europe steams full steam ahead toward implementing official discrimination by dividing society into the "good" (tested/vaccinated) and "bad" (untested/unvaccinated) people, the first ball is being thrown in the U.S. for what the ultimate goal of things like vaccine passports is: the complete removal of the "bad" people from society. The well-known journal Nature has published a call for the UN and all governments to take rock-hard measures to stop 'anti-vax aggression'. Here is how you, as an unvaccinated person, will soon be seen and treated: as a terrorist.

The fascism of murderous maniacs like Hitler and Stalin is making a full return. The Texan pediatrician Peter Hotez has become such an extreme corona idol that he puts people who are critical of vaccinations on a par with cyber criminals and nuclear terrorism. Using outright war language, he calls for a "counteroffensive" by governments to attack and silence anyone who opposes vaccinations.

'Counteroffensive against new destructive forces'

'Stopping the spread of the coronavirus requires a high-level counteroffensive against new destructive forces,' Hotez writes. 'Efforts must extend to the areas of cyber security, law enforcement, public education and international relations. A high-level inter-agency task force reporting to the UN secretary general could take stock of the overall impact of anti-vaccine aggression, and propose tough, balanced measures.'

'This task force should include experts who have tackled complex global threats such as terrorism, cyber attacks and nuclear armament. Indeed, anti-science is now approaching a similar level of threat. It is becoming increasingly clear that a counteroffensive is needed to promote vaccinations.'

Police and military against vaccine opponents

Hotez talks about "targeted attacks on scientists" allegedly committed by anti-vaxxers, but does not cite a single concrete example. To stop this fictitious "aggression," he literally advocates targeted (armed) attacks on anti-vaxxers. In fact, he wants the government to use the police and the army to deal with vaccine critics and refusers - in reality people who refuse to take part in these gene-manipulating experiments, which, according to official EU statistics, have already made enormous numbers of victims.

By placing this outrageous call, Nature, which was already completely in the pocket of the international vaccine mafia, which is now carrying out a monstrous genocidal experiment on the whole of humanity with the help of almost all governments, has lost its credibility once and for all.

Coarse violence against the 'wrong' people is considered okay again

Coarse violence against innocent men, women and children is evidently considered okay again. We have been warning for years against the return and even surpassing of the 1930s and 1940s, and now it is happening. If this isn't stopped, if people don't rise up en masse against this potential worst crime against humanity ever, it's going to end irrevocably as it did in the 1940s, namely with "facilities" where the unwanted "wrong" people are locked up and put away so that the rest of society can conduct itself "safely" again.

Or in other words: with concentration camps.

As long as people continue to deny that a repeat of this horrible history is possible, as long as people refuse to face the chilling parallels with Nazi Germany, the globalist forces of vaccination can continue unimpeded.

'The Russians' have done it again

And 'of course' also according to Hotez 'the Russians' are behind all the 'vaccine disinformation'. Then we forget for a moment that Russia was one of the first to develop a vaccine and begin administering it to its population.

No matter, because since last year the Western media have also definitively thrown off their last shred of feigned independence and objectivity, and are even proud to function as the propaganda organs of the Western establishment and the globalist climate-vaccine cult. By the way, we have been writing for years that "the Russians" will be blamed for just about everything, and that has the purpose of getting you to agree to - even call for - the planned Third World War against Russia, and most likely against China as well.

Humanity ruled by unscrupulous monsters

Unscrupulous monsters are at the helm of humanity, which, through blind obedience and unconditional docility, is itself being turned step by step into an equally unscrupulous monster. It is not yet too late, but there is very little time left to stop mandatory testing and vaccination passports, followed by mandatory testing and vaccinations, and then the imprisonment and eventual removal of the "wrong" unvaccinated - in Hotez' eyes the new "terrorists".

Chapter 12: Killer jabs?

Low concentrations of spike protein have already changed the respiratory and immunological systems of vaccinated people - Indications that vaccinated people may be a hazard to unvaccinated individuals are becoming stronger –

A government that cares about your health would suspend vaccinations right away.

Criticism of the Covid-19 vaccines is also swelling from established active science.

Dr. Lee Makowski, chair of the bioengineering department at Northeastern University, warns in the journal Viruses that there is growing evidence that the spike protein, which is produced by the human body at the instruction of ALL corona vaccines, can cause major health damage and even death.

Politicians, media, and agencies such as the CDC and the WHF claim that the spike protein is "harmless," and the Covid vaccines that cause the body to produce this protein are "safe.

However, a growing number of established active scientists are seeing more and more evidence and proof that just the opposite is true.

'Damage, serious infections and death from these vaccines?'

The title of Dr. Makowski's article in the journal Viruses says it all:

'Do Covid vaccines designed to create immunity to the spike protein instead cause harm, serious infections and death?'

The researchers found that even at low concentrations, the spike protein induces genetic changes in the respiratory tract, and directly affects the immune system's response to inflammation and viruses. In fact, according to Dr. Makowski, it seems that only the spike protein is responsible for the now infamous blood clots, rather than the (supposed) SARS-CoV-2 virus itself.

If this is confirmed by more scientists, then the Covid-19 vaccines - which regardless of their mode of action (mRNA, adenovirus/viral vector, DNA) all code for the spike protein - are even more dangerous to human health than critical scientists have already suspected since last year.

Are vaccinated people becoming walking infection hotspots?

Moreover, it is becoming plausible that Dr. Lee Merritt may well be right, and the spike protein produced in vaccinated people is transmissible to others. In other words, vaccinated people become walking spike factories, and thus could also infect unvaccinated people with a harmful, potentially deadly autoimmune disease.

Scientists at the Sloan Kettering Institute sound another, equally dire warning: the mRNA in the vaccines can cause proteins that prevent the development of cancer to be suppressed. Thus, the Covid vaccines increase the risk of getting cancer.

UCLA Dr. Whelan warned FDA of serious health damage

In December 2020, Dr. J. Patrick Whelan of UCLA warned the U.S. FDA that the "viral spike protein that is the target of the important Covid vaccines is also one of the major substances causing damage to more distant organs, possibly including the heart, lungs and kidneys.

Dr. Whelan explained that it is not the virus, but the spike protein that is responsible for some people having such a difficult time recovering from Covid-19, and often continuing to have long-term health problems, including heart problems.

This is because the spike protein binds to ACE-2 receptors in the heart, and also in the brain and other organs such as the liver and kidneys. This can damage even the smallest blood vessels.

Whelan has therefore made it clear to the FDA that the spike protein "in" the vaccines causes serious health problems.

Pathologists and dentists also point to spike protein as a culprit

Dr. Richard Vander Heide, professor of pathology at Louisiana State University, performed autopsies on Covid-19 deaths and came to the same conclusion: the blood clots, which some of the deceased are full of, are caused by the spike protein.

Overweight people are especially at risk, as they often suffer from chronic inflammation.

Even dentists are sounding the alarm. They see previously healthy patients now getting gum inflammation, and think the spike protein is the culprit.

Pfizer is even experimenting on children, toddlers and babies

A 40-year-old California pregnancy medicine physician described the first dose of the Pfizer vaccine in a patient as "killing the fetus," causing the woman to miscarry six days later.

Meanwhile, vaccine manufacturer Pfizer continues to demonstrate that it no longer has any ethical boundaries.

70

Even children are now being used as guinea pigs for their experimental gene therapy 'vaccines'. A two-year-old toddler has already died from it.

Known for years that mRNA can be inhaled

It has been known for years that mRNA can be exhaled and inhaled, and in this way can serve as a passive vaccine. 'Does this mean that the Covid spike protein, which is produced by the human body after it has been vaccinated, can escape through the breath and infect unvaccinated people?' wonders Dr Mark Sircus, professor of natural oncology.

'It's a terrible thought that the lunatics who created the virus with 'gain of function' experiments are going hand in hand with similar lunatics in the pharmaceutical industry who are using their vaccine to spread spike proteins even more widely throughout the human population.'

A government that has your health at heart would stop vaccinating immediately

It seems obvious to me that any government that actually has the health of the people at heart would declare a moratorium on all Covid vaccinations right now, at least until more research has been done worldwide, before these vaccines indeed end in a deadly slaughter the likes of which the world has never seen before.

However, the opposite is true. The European government is working on a series of (constitutional) amendments that should make the taking away of our freedom and right of self-determination permanent, as well as pave the way for mandatory vaccinations.

Should it indeed come to this, then we can probably only conclude that our own government has declared itself the greatest enemy of public health, and is knowingly helping to carry out a potential genocide. We can only hope that there are enough politicians and parliamentarians in Brussels who will (again) listen to their conscience. A number of policy makers seem to have definitively lost their ability to do so.

Chapter 13: Immune system suppression

Covid-19 is "mainly a vascular illness," according to researchers - Circulation Research: Lung injury is aided by spike protein - Your immune system is working against you to protect you from the vaccine.

In a scientific publication, researchers at the famed Salk Institute, which was founded by vaccine pioneer Jonas Salk, indirectly admit that the Covid vaccinations induce life-threatening blood clots and harm to both blood vessels and the immune system.

We noted earlier this week that an increasing number of well-known scientists are coming to the opinion that vaccines are the greatest hazard to human health.

Thousands of Europeans and Americans have already paid with their lives, and hundreds of thousands with their health, for their "voluntary" participation in history's greatest "medical" experiment.

In the West, all Covid vaccinations program the human body to create the spike protein, the most lethal element of the alleged SARS-CoV-2 virus, with the goal of shielding humans against the spike protein's damaging consequences.

In a nutshell, we make your body manufacture something harmful in order for it to generate antibodies against that same danger, but we have no idea how or if this process will ever be stopped.

So why not take the "risk" of getting the virus, which has been shown to not make 99.7% of the population sick, if at all? No, in 2021, that rational, historically uncontroversial line of reasoning is suddenly so antiquated. We can no longer rely on our natural immune system and must instead rely on what is administered through a syringe.

'Covid-19 is mostly a vascular illness,' says the researcher.

The vaccination industry, politicians, and the media continue to insist that the spike protein is safe, but the Salk Institute has now established that this is not the case. On the contrary, the Salk researchers and other scientific colleagues warn in the publication "The spike protein of the new coronavirus plays an extra crucial role in disease" that the spike protein harms cells, "confirming that Covid-19 is largely a vascular illness."

Another spike protein that has claimed so many lives?

Of course, the Salk scientists are forbidden from criticizing vaccines directly. That is why, according to their article, the spike protein produced by vaccines behaves quite differently than the spike protein produced by the alleged virus.

To begin with, this contradicts all vaccine makers' claims that their vaccines create the same spike protein. Second, it casts doubt on the efficacy of vaccines, because if the spike protein produced by vaccines differs significantly from that produced by the virus, what is the point of vaccination (assuming, for the time being, that these genetically designed 'vaccines' operate at all)?

On the plus side, even pro-vaccine scientists now accept that the spike protein is to blame for a large number of deaths and people suffering from major side effects and long-term, often permanent health harm. In other words, it's an implied admission that Covid-19 vaccinations are potentially fatal.

Spike protein causes lung injury, according to research published in Circulation Research.

"The SARS-Cov-2 spike protein impairs endothelial function by inhibiting ACE-2," according to a scientific study published in Circulation Research. The inside of the heart and blood vessels are lined with edothele cells. By decreasing ACE-2 receptors, the spike protein 'promotes lung injury.' The endothelial cells in blood arteries are damaged, and the metabolism is disrupted as a result.

The authors of this study were also pro-vaccination, claiming that "vaccine-generated antibodies" may protect the body from the spike protein. Essentially, the spike protein can cause significant damage to vascular cells, and the immune system can counteract this damage by fighting the spike protein.

The immune system is trying to protect you AGAINST the vaccine

In other words, the human immune system strives to defend the patient from the vaccine's negative effects and counter-reactions in order to prevent the patient from dying. Anyone who survives the Covid vaccine owes it to their own immune system's protection AGAINST the vaccine, not the vaccination itself.

'The vaccination is the weapon,' Mike 'Natural News' Adams concludes. 'Your immune system protects you. All Covid vaccinations should be withdrawn off the market immediately and re-evaluated for long-term negative effects based on this research alone.'

According to official VAERS statistics, the number of vaccine-related deaths in the United States in 2021 will be almost 4000 percent more than the total number of vaccine-related deaths in 2020.

The holy vaccine is not to blame for a heart attack or a cerebral hemorrhage.

The following mechanism has been scientifically proved and is now established: the Covid-19 vaccinations encourage your body to make the spike protein, which can cause vascular damage and blood clots, which can move throughout the body and end up in various organs (heart, lungs, brain, etc.). People who die as a result of this are referred to as having had a "heart attack," "blood clot," or "brain haemorrhage" - the sacrosanct vaccines can and must never be blamed, no matter how much evidence there is today showing they are the main reasons.

Vaccine recipients appear to offer a risk to the unvaccinated, in addition to the possibility for permanent or deadly harm to their own health. Many of the corona'wappies' who have recently had their shots have been transformed into walking'spike factories,' and can now exhale these spike proteins. They can so infect others through this 'shedding' process.

Bioweapon vaccines were created by the apartheid administration against the black population.

Vaccines have long been used as bioweapons against the general public. South Africa's Apartheid Government created the technology underlying such a "self-replicating" vaccination. Scientists were developing 'racial' vaccines at the time, with the goal of eradicating much of the black population.

This year, the Johns Hopkins Bloomberg School of Public Health proposed using a self-replicating vaccine to automatically 'vaccinate' the whole world's population.

Drones and AI robots would subsequently be used to enforce and monitor the program.

People who are still eager to sign up in a vaccine alley to be genetically modified to generate a potentially life-threatening spike protein appear to have been fully misled by the mainstream media and system politicians. They've been numb to all the warnings and the mountains of proof, and they can't believe the world is being ruled by unscrupulous monsters who have no qualms about committing the potentially single biggest genocide in human history.

Chapter 14: Passports & chips

A 2016 interview with WEF senior executive Klaus Schwab, in which he predicts that "within 10 years" an obligatory global health card will be adopted, and everyone will have implanted microchips, adds to the proof that the Covid-19 issue was painstakingly prepared.

Schwab was reportedly working on a plan at least five years ago to create a huge virus outbreak and exploit it to establish health passports and link them to mandatory testing and vaccinations, all according to the problem-reaction-solution approach. The goal is to have complete control over the whole human population on the planet.

'Within 10 years, we will have implanted microchips,' said Schwab five years ago.

In 2016, a French-speaking interviewer asked him, 'Are we talking about implantable chips?' 'When is it going to happen?'

'Absolutely in the next ten years,' said Schwab. 'We'll start by putting them in our clothes.' We can next picture implanting them in our brains or skin.' The WEF foreman then commented on his vision of man and machine 'fusing.'

'In the future, we may be able to communicate directly between our brains and the digital world.' We observe a merger of the physical, digital, and biological worlds.' People will simply have to think about someone in the future to be able to reach them straight through the 'cloud.'

There will be no more biological persons with natural DNA in the transhumanist world, which will finally become fully "digital." The 'cloud' will be used to store everyone's data.

Humanity has begun to be reprogrammed genetically.

The current economic order will be destroyed by Schwab's 'Great Reset' ('Build Back Better'). The looming financial meltdown will be exploited to launch a new global system based only on digital money and transactions. This new system will be connected to the entire world thanks to 5G technology. Refusers will be barred from "buying and selling," in other words, from social life.

In the late 2020s, Covid-19 mRNA 'vaccines' began genetically programming and manipulating humanity in order to make it 'fit' to be first linked, then integrated, with this global digital system, which, as you know, I believe is the Biblical realm of 'the Beast.'

These gene-altering vaccines have the potential to eliminate your free will and ability to think for yourself, as well as your desire and ability to connect with the spiritual realm.

Christian Perspective: Humanity is cut off from God

From a Christian perspective, the reprogramming of human DNA through these vaccines can be seen as Satan's final attempt to permanently separate humankind from God. This appears to be the true explanation for the prophetic Bible book of Revelation's warning that individuals who bear this "mark" will perish.

This isn't simply because of a chip and a succession of pricks; it's because of what those pricks will do to and in you. As a result, God will be unable to save those whose minds (free will) have been reprogrammed to total obedience ('worship'). That will necessitate His intervention, for otherwise, humanity as a whole will be lost forever.

False teachings have blinded a large portion of Christianity.

The essential aspect of this devious plot, which has been in the works for a long time, was the infiltration of Christianity with a series of false teachings, with the goal of keeping believers blind until the end of time in preparation for the advent and establishment of the Beast's rule.

Indeed, tens to hundreds of millions of Christians, particularly in the West, believe that they will never have to live through this period. Even now, when the implementation of this system has begun, the majority of people refuse to accept it. With their pro-vaccination views, most Christian parties and churches are openly cooperating in this "Great Reset" to the domain of "the Beast." In theological terms, the Vatican is the most powerful and convinced driver of this.

'But we were duped!' isn't an excuse.

Perhaps a biblical parallel can help some people understand? Genesis 3, the tale of creation and the 'Fall,' as told to us today: The serpent persuaded Adam and Eve that they were not allowed to 'eat' the 'apple,' in this case the sign, i.e. not to have it pricked in them (root test of 'the sign': charagma = scratch/something with a needle = prick), but the serpent persuaded them that this sign would not damn them, but rather make them into 'gods.' After being persuaded by this falsehood, their complaints against God ('but we've been lied to!') were futile, and they died slowly and painfully. They could have and should have known, thus they had no justification.

Accepting 'the sign,' according to the Bible, carries an even worse consequence: eternal death. Allowing yourself to be genetically modified with mRNA vaccinations and then integrated into a global digital network, so relinquishing all control over your body and free will, will be up to each individual to decide whether the danger is worth it.

Chapter 15: Endless debt?

The pandemic fraud has dragged the West further into debt than WW2 - Britain's largest pension fund (No. 6 in the world) tells investors that withdrawing money may take up to 95 days, and warns of probable insolvency.

The impending financial system collapse is the secret driver of the continuation of the corona pandemic fake measures and the frightening developments in Ukraine. Actually, this is the same problem that existed from 2008 to 2011, since it was only "fixed" with negative interest rates and massive sums of new digital money, which benefited mainly governments, shareholders, and large financial players. Now that the IMF has warned in a study that government debts have never been so high since WWII, this mega catastrophe, which will have far-reaching effects for ordinary people, might erupt at any time.

We've been writing about this for years, and now the IMF is warning that national debts have never been so high since World War II. The Corona crisis has been utilized as an excuse worldwide to practically create 'money like water,' because it is now worth nothing. The entire amount involved in Europe alone is a monstrous €130 billion, or almost one-third of the total national debt until 2019.

The New Great Depression has only been postponed.

If half of the economy had not been put on a drip since last year, we would currently be in a deeper Depression than the 1930s. So, what do you think is a good solution? Try to recall your first high school economics lesson, or the question that nearly every child has asked their parents at some point in their lives: "Why don't we just put money on the copy machine so that we always have enough and can buy copies?" "wealthy

We're assuming we don't have to answer these questions? If that's the case, you should stop reading and return to the mainstream propaganda media, which appears to have no idea what's going on (and if they did, they may not write about it until the crisis is a fait accompli and irreversible fact).

Is the crisis resolved? Greece's debt has already reached 200 percent of GDP.

The newest IMF 'Fiscal Monitor' report offers a bleak picture: government debts have never been proportionally so high since the end of WW2, the deadliest conflict ever fought. Do you recall the Greek crisis, which jeopardized the whole Eurozone and EU and was only just averted? Greece's federal debt has climbed to 160 percent of GDP. The country had to be'rescued' with several rescue packages totaling hundreds of billions of euros from countries such as the Germany.

Greece's national debt has now risen to more than 200 percent of GDP. What do you think, did this'rescue' help?

At least not for the Greek people or the Greek economy. They simply received crumbs. The only ones "saved" were the European banks, who were "paid" by the European taxpayer for their debts to Greece in this especially deceptive manner. In the media, we were informed that we had'rescued' the Greeks, but in reality, just like in 2008, we had saved the banks - the exact ones who had gotten us into this mess.

For example, the number of IC beds has been cut in half, resulting in Europe's lowest per capita level. Then, in 2020, a flu-like respiratory virus arose, the threat of which was purposely inflated in order to push through all sorts of punitive freedom-restricting restrictions. We do it for the sake of caring (after we have wrecked it first)'. No, 'we' do it to prepare the populace for a bank crisis-lockdown.

Banks must be bailed out again.

It is now 2021, and the banks must be saved once more. As we have previously stated, Europe's major systemic banks, such as Deutsche Bank and Société Générale, are technically bankrupt. At the same time, the pandemic myth has driven industrialized countries deeper into debt than World War II did, and the ECB has lately taken further moves that further erode our purchasing power and wealth.

Nobody is talking about the need to get out of debt anymore. All parties - governments and corporations - hope that interest rates will remain zero or negative in perpetuity, and that money will continue to play no role in the state. An increase in interest rates is, indeed, the worst-case situation. Even if it is minor, it will quickly force two much larger European debt nations, Italy and Spain, into state bankruptcy. Rescue is out of the question since it would cost trillions of euros. As a result, the collapse of any of these two countries automatically entails the collapse of the eurozone.

'Reorganization contributions,' but from whom?

As a result, the IMF suggests that nations begin levying 'clean-up payments' on incomes, assets, and earnings - a somewhat perplexing advice, considering that only robust and sustained economic development can potentially bring us back from the brink of this systemic disaster. If you then tax the already distressed business sector even more harshly, you will only have the opposite effect: the crisis will be exacerbated and intensified, hundreds of thousands of businesses will fail, and countless people will lose their jobs.

And there is nothing more to be gotten from the already strained people. Even higher taxes and even deeper cutbacks will drive significant swaths of the poor and middle classes into abject poverty. Governments have no choice but to turn to draconian financial repression, which will hurt the ordinary citizen, but notably the lowest-paid and most vulnerable. Millions of people will soon be unable to afford their housing/energy bills and foodstuffs on their own. Most of us will have to tighten our belts both metaphorically and practically.

Some analysts predict "Weimar"-style hyperinflation, which will utterly deplete our purchasing power. Given the current extremely perilous circumstances for many residents and businesses, even a considerably lower inflation rate of 3% to 4% will be the ultimate blow. Government bonds, life insurance, pension money, and savings will be worthless in no time.

The world's sixth insurer has issued a 'insolvency' warning.

Signs that the financial system crisis is approaching are also obvious in the United Kingdom, where Aviva, the country's largest insurer/pension fund and the world's sixth, has notified its clients that it might take up to 95 days before they may withdraw money from their accounts.

Even more frightening is the direct warning that " If a bank/insurer/pension fund employs that phrase at all, it is a signal of exceedingly significant, most probable insurmountable difficulties.

Gold, silver, and currency have been eliminated from the United Kingdom.

Without explanation, a large sum of gold, silver, and cash was unexpectedly withdrawn from the United Kingdom and transported to Qatar recently. The Bank of International Settlements (the BIS bank in Basel, the "central bank of central banks") documented a $1.8 billion payment from the Hillary Clinton Foundation to the Qatari Central Bank (QCB).

Possible causes vary from the UK's impending financial collapse to a conflict with Russia in which British towns may be annihilated with nuclear weapons.

Citizens and businesses will own NOTHING in the digital eurozone.

We've been warning for years that a systemic catastrophe is on the way, and it appears to be almost here. This catastrophe, which might be precipitated by a false flag cyber-attack (allegedly by Russia?), would be used to push through the 'Great Reset,' which is nothing more than the installation of an unprecedentedly harsh and exceedingly draconian technocratic communist climate-vaccine tyranny.

In financial and economic terms, this implies that the euro will be totally digital, that EVERYTHING will be state-owned (even your own body), and that citizens and businesses will be forever bereft of any kind of property or voice in the issue. The World Economic Forum also expects a permanent unemployment rate of 35 percent to 41 percent, as well as the implementation of a basic income that will be just enough to keep people alive.

Do you want the great reset?

This is what is coming, and it cannot be stopped. Even if the mass of the people woke up at the last minute and revolted against this, a 'Great Reset' would still be required, but of a completely different magnitude than that of the WEF and the globalists in Washington, Brussels, London, Paris, Berlin, Rome, and The Hague. Their reset concentrates all power and riches in the hands of a small elite club, whilst the Reset that we truly require achieves the reverse.

The technically insolvent Deutsche Bank has warned that the EU's 'Green Deal,' which is intended to enable the 'Great Reset,' will really trigger a mega-crisis and herald the entrance of an eco-dictatorship that would destroy our current affluence.

In any case, last years, the European people overwhelmingly voted for parties that want to adopt, and are currently implementing, the EU's Green Deal and the World Economic Forum's Reset initiative (at least, if the election results are correct). When their false promises and visions of a technocratic climate paradise turn out to have unleashed a veritable hell on earth for almost everyone, looking in the mirror and asking yourself in bewilderment "how did we ever let it get this far?" will be the only thing left for this gullible and apathetic people with their insufferable slave mentality.

We apologize for concluding this way, but as we observe more and more individuals wearing mouth caps even outside in the sun, there is just no reason to believe that sobriety and common sense will ever return to normal. I'm concerned that this inky dark spirit of purposefully cultivated and fanned societal fear of death and insanity will only go after a great deal of sorrow and sorrow.

Chapter 16: No more money?

The impending financial mega-crisis will be exploited to complete the communist 'Great Reset.'

While the attention of both the government and the media remains almost totally on Corona, highly disturbing changes in the EU are going place in the background, which are likely to have far-reaching ramifications for our economic and buying power in the short to medium term. Because interest rates on government bonds have begun to climb again, the ECB will purchase more government debt in the coming months. Furthermore, the de facto technically bankrupt financial sector is in much more difficulties as a result of the fabricated monetary crisis. 'The only thing keeping the European Commission together any more is the ECB's magical money tree,' argues expert Alasdair Macleod. If you've ever attended two economics classes, you should know where such a thing is ""Money Tree" ALWAYS leads to: "This is a horror show in the making."

The EUSSR is a done deal, both politically and financially.

Critics sometimes refer to the European Union as the EUSSR, and by 2021, none of that is an exaggeration - rather the reverse. Politically, the EU has long functioned in the same way as the former Soviet Union: the Politburo, an unelected club of bureaucrats known as the European Commission, determines policy and sends its 'wishes' (=orders) to the European Council of Heads of Government, who debate them for show and then send these orders to their own - in name only - independent countries, where the parliaments are elected.

To maintain the pretense of a European democracy, the EU maintains its own "parliament," in which all members are paid exorbitant salaries, bonuses, and pensions for participating in this grand spectacle while maintaining mute about the fact that they have nothing, absolutely nothing to contribute. The only time this parliament appeared to have any 'power' was when it sent a European Commission home, but it was most likely staged, especially in retrospect, because it was at that time that the European people began to wake up to the EU 'socialist' (in the Marxist sense) character and purpose.

Recently, the ECB discreetly took the next step toward the euro's, the euro/Target-2 system's, and its own demise. Contrary to previous pronouncements, the bank has chosen to acquire more government bonds in the coming months as interest rates rise globally. If this tendency continues, the entire eurozone network will go bankrupt. 'And that network is a mouthful of rotting apples,' Macleod adds. 'It is the outcome of not only a broken system, but also of measures designed to keep Spain's interest rates from rising in 2012.'

'Whatever it takes,' the euro is 'saved' at the expense of citizens.

At the time, ECB President Mario Draghi famously stated that he would rescue the euro "whatever it takes." What he didn't tell us was that the cost of this "whatever it takes" will be borne by European savers and pension funds. Because of the growing debt, Christine Lagarde's action must be considerably bigger than that of her predecessor, Mario Draghi. Ultimately, all Europeans will have to pay a high price for this, in the form of a significant and irreversible loss of buying power and wealth. The EU member states' glitzy years of prosperity are coming to an end.

Lagarde kicks Draghi's 'whatever it takes' mantra up a notch. The ECB, which professes to be "independent" but is fundamentally a political organization, has always served one purpose: to ensure that the unrestrained spending of the southern member states, in particular, is always covered.

For this goal, an inventive mechanism was devised: Italy and Spain alone owe the ECB system about €1 trillion. Germany, Luxembourg, Finland, and the Netherlands, on the other hand, are owed around € 1.6 trillion under this system, with Germany owing the lion's share (more than € 1 trillion). (In reality, tiny Luxembourg may be viewed as a bank masquerading as an independent state, one of the numerous gimmicks employed by the

ECB to make the EU's financial condition appear more favorable.)

Large mega-banks are technically bankrupt.

By purchasing government bonds, the ECB has already amassed a debt of € 345 billion, owing in part to the clandestine funding of France's rising government deficit. France is now one of the PIIGS countries, although this will never be formally acknowledged because France is seen as a 'systemically important' state. Meanwhile, France's liabilities are beginning to weigh hard on the euro system, not least since the French mega-bank Société Générale, as well as Deutsche Bank and Italy's Unicredit, are technically functionally insolvent.

What the figures do not reveal is that the Bundesbank has already purchased billions of euros of German government debt on behalf of the ECB. The ever-increasing imbalance in the Target-2 system has arisen as a result of Italy, Spain, Greece, and Portugal, in particular, being saddled with an increasing number of 'bad' loans, or loans that can and will never be repaid. As a result, the 'zombie' financial systems in these nations had to be permanently fed by the ECB.

Bad loans and bad assets

The bad loans and other 'bad assets' were transferred to the euro system (and therefore, in particular, to

Germany, Finland, the Netherlands, and Luxembourg) during the 'bailout' of Greece, and subsequently to the Target-2 system during the 'bailout' of the Italian banks, which was disguised from the public. What is not included in the numbers is an even larger sum of €8.31 trillion (possibly more than €10 trillion) in short-term funding, which is basically non-existent in the eurozone.

In summary, if you have an average yearly salary of € 36,000, you can acquire a € 1 million loan from a bank without batting an eye, and the bank manager then says to you: "See what you can pay back, and when..." What do you think? Will this bank be able to survive for a long time? And can a central bank that then keeps these banks afloat for years be able to maintain its health for a long time?

'Like a group of drunks attempting to raise themselves staggeringly out of the gutter, European bank stock values have climbed alongside the markets. 'However, their ratings continue to be appallingly low,' says Macleod. The situation has deteriorated to the point that if one large eurozone bank fails, the entire system would fall like a house of cards.

The EU is a collapsing state, and its purchasing power will be wiped out.

The EU is showing all of the hallmarks of a crumbling state "the analyst continues This was most clear in the EU's reaction to Brexit, which can only be defined as stupid and infantile vengeance, regardless of the unpleasant implications for the bloc itself. Furthermore, the EU is unlikely to escape from lockdowns this year, which means that all member countries will be forced to continue incurring massive new debt in order to keep their economies afloat. The effects of highly harmful policies will be far worse for Europe than for the United States and China.

Large swaths of the economy, particularly SMEs, are on the point of collapse. When the trends in the commodities markets (oil, metals, food, etc.) are combined with the massive growth in the money supply, the result will be a worldwide loss of buying power. Because of its own structure, policies, and actions, the EU is entirely trailing behind China's economic rebound, which is now in full gear.

'And, because the ECB is in charge of everything's finance, the EU's problem will undoubtedly begin there. It will undoubtedly bring down the majority of the financial sector... It won't take a significant increase in interest rates to wipe it away.' The genuine worth of the 'value' and 'assets' claimed by the large Eurozone banks on their balance sheets is then revealed: 'basically NOTHING.' It's no surprise that capital flight from the Eurozone has increased. Money usually exits nations with terrible and wasteful policies, and it will soon be worthless.

'The system is purposely inflated in order to accomplish the communist Great Reset.'

If you're wondering, why aren't they doing something to avoid this? Then we'll respond: because, in our opinion, the system is being deliberately blown apart. A digital euro is already in the works, and it will eventually replace all currency. This new digital money system will most likely be launched during or shortly after the approaching financial mega-crisis, and will be gradually connected to everything (ID/passport, debit card, Covid card, and so on). All debts will be forfeited, and all 'assets,' all property, all funds, of all corporations and people, will be transferred to the state.

The 'Great Reset,' or the change of the once-successful E.E.C. free trade bloc into a European Soviet Union with a technocratic and profoundly communist regime, will then be completed. Then our prosperity, as well as all of our liberties and belongings, will be restored. (And you, as an entrepreneur, were overjoyed when the government pledged to reimburse you for 100 percent of your fixed expenditures! Do you honestly not know you've all walked right into a trap? That you will soon have nothing more to say regarding your own business and survival in this controlled economy?)

Look through the history books to gain a sense of how 'nice' life will be for us then. However, for the vast majority of people, such an appeal will fall on deaf ears. They voted even more heavily for allegedly 'liberal' parties that have for years adopted virtually entirely neo-Marxist EU policies.

To our great dismay, there appears to be just one thing left to do to bring the people back to their senses, and that is to experience a lot of suffering (again). With the hope that our surviving (grand)children will have learnt from these harsh lessons and will be able and willing to construct a far healthier society, a world where Big Banks, Big Pharma, Big Tech, Big Military, and Big Government, in other words: Big Corruption, have no place.

Chapter 17: 1921-1922?

The parallel between Germany 1914-1923 and the West 2010-2021 is seamless.

Is history repeating itself in every way, but on an even larger scale? It looks suspiciously like it. Just as in the 1910s - 1920s, unimaginable amounts of money created out of thin air have been used to buy up massive amounts of debt and create enormous wealth, and everyone wants a piece of the pie. Wall Street chief Michael Burry, nicknamed 'Big Short' because he was the first investor to foresee the subprime crisis (2007-2010), warns that hyperinflation will suddenly break out, just as it did in the Weimar Republic.

'People have said I didn't warn last time,' hedge fund manager 'Big Short' Burry responded to the storm of reactions to his hyperinflation prediction. *'I did, but nobody listened. So I'm warning now. And again, no one listens. But I will have proof that I warned.'*

Recently, Burry tweeted that the US government's MMT (Modern Monetary Theory, the de facto communist course that has been followed in the EU for some 7 years) 'invites inflation'. The Biden administration is spending trillions to keep the economy and society 'afloat' in the midst of the corona crisis, but will achieve the opposite as soon as they are gradually opened again. When demand rises again, all that money will explode the prices and costs of workers, which will be the beginning of inflation, or hyperinflation, spiraling out of control.

'It couldn't go on'

Bank of America CIO Michael Hartnett also compares the 'tsunami of fiscal stimulus' and monetization of the huge debt burden (which has been done in the EU since 2014 with massive buybacks of sovereign debt and with negative interest rates, at the expense of savings, pensions and purchasing power) directly to the situation in Germany (the Weimar Republic) after World War I.

Jens Parsson wrote in 1974 that the period 1914 - 1923 was characterized by "great prosperity, at least for those profiting from the 'boom.' There was a 'can't wait' atmosphere. Prices were stable, and the stock market and business were doing fine. The German Mark even initially became worth more than the dollar, and for a while was the strongest currency in the world.

Yet there were "simultaneous groups with poverty. More and more people fell out of the easy money, and could not get into it. Crime rose sharply.' The common man 'became demoralized', because hard work and saving yielded less and less, while others grew their money from their lazy lounger, and became puissant rich.

Everyone wanted a piece of the pie

Almost any form of enterprise, no matter how speculative, made money. The number of collapses and bankruptcies fell. The 'natural (economic) selection', whereby weak, badly run and/or non-essential companies fall and the stronger ones stay afloat, disappeared.

Speculation became one of the most important activities in Germany. Everyone wanted a piece of the pie, including citizens of almost all classes. Even elevator operators took part in investing. It was not production, innovation and achievement that created prosperity, but money and speculation. The Berlin stock exchange literally could not keep up with the volumes of securities traded.

1921/22 = 2021/22

And then came the blow, as sudden as it was devastating. All the marks that existed in the world in 1922 were not enough in November 1923 to buy a single newspaper or a ticket for the streetcar. 'That was the spectacular part of the collapse, but most of the real loss in (monetary) wealth had occurred much earlier. During these years, the structure quietly built itself up for this blow. The German inflation cycle lasted not one, but 9 years: 8 years of growth, and only 1 year of collapse.

You must have had your eyes closed very tightly for the past 10+ years to deny that Burry is doubly right when he writes that this 47-year-old analysis applies seamlessly to the 2010 - 2021 period, in which dollars (and euros) 'could just as easily have fallen from the sky... management teams got creative and took even more risks... and paid out debt-financed dividends to investors, or invested in risky growth opportunities.'

Citizens were massively invited and urged to invest their own money, just as they were then, because stock prices would only continue to rise anyway, as would house prices. In recent years, the highly speculative crypto market turned out to be the most profitable; some people who got in early became very rich, and were able to retire early.

And again we are on the brink of an unprecedented crash

As in 1921-1922, most people do not realize that exactly a century later, thanks to even worse speculative fever and unprecedentedly insane fiscal and monetary policies, we are once again on the verge of such a sudden huge crash, Burry also warns. The 'Weimar' hyperinflation wiped out all prosperity in no time, except that of the 'elite' and a few major financial players. Bitter poverty and misery awaited the people, which became the fertile ground for the rise of the Nazis.

And there are more chilling parallels. Just as in the 1930s, in our time there has been mass fear-mongering, people have been pitted against each other, and harsh dictatorial measures have been taken that have ended our freedoms and many of our rights. Just as in the 1940s, medical experiments are being conducted on people, but now not just in closed camps, but worldwide, with controversial vaccinations, on billions at a time. And just like in the 1920s, most people didn't want to hear about a crisis; after all, the trees were growing to the sky, and they would always continue to do so.

However, politicians have long been aware that the biggest financial crisis of all time is imminent. In order to nip mass panic and protests in the bud, a common respiratory virus was chosen as the pretext to destroy the freedoms and rights of citizens step by step. We wrote from the beginning that the curfew has nothing to do with public health and safety, but everything to do with capitalizing on this impending crisis. And what do you think? Meanwhile, there is speculation in The Hague about possibly extending the curfew to noon, "should that be necessary.

Is there escape from this 'Great Reset'?

Count on it that it WILL be necessary, however not for a viral mutation, as will again be falsely claimed, but to keep the people locked up in their carefully crafted emergency measures and laws, so that they cannot revolt en masse when it turns out that almost everything they took for granted to hold 'value' forever - including their purchasing power, homes, jobs, investments and pensions - is gone for good, and this will have been done on purpose too, because it carries out a political-ideological agenda: the 'Great Reset'.

Is there an escape, an alternative? Yes, but only if we peacefully resist by refusing en masse to continue to contribute to our own demise.

Chapter 18: Hyperinflation

For years, we have been amazed that most people seem to believe it is normal for central banks to continue creating unimaginable amounts of money out of thin air at the push of a button so that governments can continue to spend massive amounts of money while believing that their purchasing power will be maintained.

Anyone who has taken two economics classes in high school knows that this is against all financial and fiscal laws, and it will result in a play sooner or later. It's almost here: the Bank of America announces HYPERinflation. This means that the currency's value will plummet, and the costs of most products and services would skyrocket.

According to annual estimates, the number of US corporations reporting (high) inflation has climbed by about 800%. As a result, Bank of America cannot help but notice this "At the very least, it suggests that 'temporary' hyperinflation is on the way.

Commodities (+28%), consumer prices (+36%), transportation (+35%), and manufactured products (+35%) are particularly vulnerable to price increases. Although the BoA believes it will remain'manageable,' hyperinflation is a process that intrinsically shows that something is spiraling out of control.

Exorbitant prices

This means that, among other things, citizens will eventually have to pay significantly more for almost everything at an escalating rate. Actually, we can observe this disguised high inflation in the increasing property prices (after all, these are not associated with a strong economic recovery, but with a government-funded debt economy). Furthermore, an increasing number of consumers are complaining that their weekly shopping have grown significantly more expensive in a relatively short period of time.

The end of prosperity is now in sight.

As depressing as it may be to read, the end of Western affluence is now in sight. Indeed, the situation in Europe is not dissimilar to that in the United States, and in some ways is far worse.

Consider the seemingly endless sovereign debts of Italy, Greece, and Spain, as well as France and Belgium. Furthermore, large European systemic banks like Deutsche Bank, Société Générale, and UniCredit are technically bankrupt.

The Green Deal and the Great Reset

On top of that, the EU's "Green Deal" and the World Economic Forum's "Excellent Reset. The former will make energy, transportation, and food virtually unaffordable for millions of people, while the latter will permanently erase the few vestiges of freedom and self-determination we have left, putting 35 to 41 percent of people out of work, according to WEF data.

While the West is tearing itself apart as a result of the realization of this climate dystopia, China and Russia have already begun to seize the baton from us.

Chapter 19: Imminent depopulation

MERS-CoV had a 40% mortality rate in 2012 - African variant made contagious to humans through genetic engineering - Repeat of 2020, supplemented by mandatory testing and mandatory vaccinations for all? - Predictable: politics and media will blame unvaccinated people

Exactly according to the scenario we have described many times since last year, medical journals are announcing the next pandemic now that Covid-19 seems to be on its way out: MERS-CoV. We can therefore expect a repeat of everything from last year's deliberate scare-mongering to the disinformation propaganda in the mainstream media and a rush to the health care system, after which 'natural' measures will be taken such as new strict lockdowns, supplemented by mandatory testing and mandatory vaccinations for everyone. Because again, the main intention of this pandemic seems to be to inject everyone with yet another series of new experimental vaccines.

'Make no mistake, this will not be the last time the world faces the threat of a pandemic,' Tedros told the UN General Assembly of the health ministers of the 194 member states earlier this year. 'It is an evolutionary certainty that there will be another virus with the potential to be even more infectious and deadly than this one.'

Indeed, that other virus could already be coming. An international team of researchers has discovered that Middle East Respiratory Syndrome (MERS) is just a few mutations away from becoming a serious pandemic. In their paper, published in Proceedings of the National Academy of Sciences, they describe their research on several MERS variants.

MERS-CoV first surfaced in Saudi Arabia in 2012, and is said to be particularly deadly. About 40% of the first patients died from their infections, which were allegedly caused mainly by infected dromedaries. And coincidence or not, evidence was also found that bats had infected the camels. According to researchers, 80% of all dromedaries tested (70% live in Africa) now have antibodies in their blood.

African variant made contagious to humans through genetic engineering

The outbreak of MERS-CoV did not receive much attention because there would be no human-to-human contamination. The scientists investigated why not many more Africans - given their many interactions with dromedaries - had not become infected. There, the virus circulates primarily in dromedaries in Morocco, Nigeria, Ethiopia and Burkina Faso. Samples were collected and it turned out that the variants that occur in Arabia can be easily transmitted from person to person, but not those in Africa.

The difference between the variants is in the amino acids of the S protein. By genetically modifying the African variant so that it had the same 'Arabian' amino acids, they succeeded in making the African variant more infectious to human cells as well. The big, unasked question, of course, is: why would you want to do that? Why would you want to make a virus that is (almost) harmless to humans much more infectious, as happened with the coronavirus?

Anyway, the researchers think that the reason that the variants in the Middle East have not yet mutated to infect many people is that the dromedary trade goes almost exclusively one way, from Africa to the Middle East. However, they warn that if that trade reverses at some point, or if another animal also becomes a carrier and is traded to Africa, mutations could occur that could cause a deadly pandemic. (1)

Virus in top 10 WHO

MERS-CoV is very similar to SARS-1 and also causes very severe respiratory symptoms. Among humans, it still has a 35% mortality rate. There is no treatment or vaccine yet. Since 2012, more than 2,100 people have been infected with MERS-CoV, 813 of whom have died. The virus is now in the top 10 of WHO's list of emerging diseases that should be investigated with the highest priority (2).

SPARS = MERS-CoV or SARS-3?

111

Late last year, the possible successor to Covid-19 was already announced: SPARS. In a simulation by Johns Hopkins University, this pandemic breaks out in 2025, and lasts until 2028.

'The SPARS pandemic 2025 - 2028; A Futuristic Scenario for Public Health Risk Communicators' (PDF, 2017) was a simulation similar to the later 'Event 201' in October 2019, when every detail was practiced on managing a global outbreak with a coronavirus, which, according to the working forecast, would kill 65 million people. That 'simulation', as you all know, became a reality in almost every respect (only the number of deaths, fortunately, remains far behind (yet?)).

In fact, a World Bank document states that the current 'project' called 'Covid-19 Strategic Preparedness and Response Program (SPRP)' will last until March 31, 2025. Only then will SARS-CoV-2 / Covid-19 presumably be declared definitively 'over', although Covid could therefore also be succeeded by MERS-CoV in the meantime.

After that the successor could start to appear immediately: SPARS, which is a reference to the U.S. city of St.Paul where this future coronavirus will first emerge according to the simulation. This new virus will, of course, be renamed in or around 2025, and could also start again in Asia, for example. However, it could also become SARS-3, which is already ready in an Italian laboratory.

So it is not unlikely that SPARS will actually become SARS-3 or MERS-CoV. 2025 was just a fictional year, which could just as easily become 2023 or earlier. The SPARS simulation also talked about a vaccine called COROVAX as the desired solution to stop this "pandemic," and which would be introduced in the scenario in July 2026. Three years after this 2017 document, a COROVAX vaccine was literally being developed.

This is how anti-vaxxers would be convinced

A notable similarity to SARS-CoV-2 / Covid-19 is that the fictional SPARS infection (/ MERS-CoV or SARS-3 infection?) is often followed by severe bacteriological pneumonia (pg. 57). It also describes how a well-known anti-vaxxer "sees the light" after her infant son develops severe pneumonia, and heals only after administration of regular medication. Authorities then use stories like this to convince vaccine opponents.

Striking similarity to 2020-2021: '... several influential politicians and representatives of institutions came under fire for sensationalizing the severity of the event for certain political gain... A broad social media movement, led mainly by outspoken parents of affected children, coupled with the widespread distrust of 'Big Pharma', supported the narrative that the development

113

of SPARS MCMs (vaccines) was unnecessary, and driven by some profit-seeking individuals.'

It also pointed to 'conspiracy theories' that this virus was also intentionally created, and/or deliberately unleashed on the population by the government as a bioweapon (pg. 66). Meanwhile, the 'Fauci Files', published even by American mainstream media, revealed that the coronavirus was internally called a deliberately created bioweapon as early as March 11, 2020.

Unvaccinated will soon be blamed directly

The pharmaceutical manufacturers, who have proven over the past year how extremely profitable vaccinating during a p(l)andemic can be, are busy developing new vaccines. Bloomberg pointed to GlaxoSmithKline (and partner Sanofi) in late May, which is already making the next generation of Covid vaccines. According to Roger Connor, head of vaccine development, a trial period of a new vaccine on more than 37,000 people was to begin as early as June.

Given the increasingly harsh, often shocking reactions in society to people refusing to be vaccinated against Covid-19 (calls for forced vaccinations are getting louder, and the first calls to put refusers in camps have also been heard), we think that we are long past the stage of "convincing" anti-vaxxers, and soon, if this next pandemic does indeed come, will go straight to openly

114

falsely blaming unvaccinated people by politicians and media.

Suppose that vaccines will indeed cause enormous health problems, as top scientists and other experts have been predicting for months (see our many articles on this subject). Then there will be a new run on health care and hospitals, after which harsh measures will again be taken. On TV, 'scientists' approved by the pharma-vaccine complex will claim that it is not because of the vaccines, but because of a mutation that was able to emerge thanks to the unvaccinated people.

Chapter 20: Fuel shortage

Is this a practice run for the upcoming big cyber strike on the West?

According to experts, the cyber attack on the main fuel pipeline in the United States could have been resolved in a matter of hours, and thus bears all the hallmarks of a 'false flag' operation designed to bring the American people completely to their knees before the emerging communist UN/WEF climate-vaccine dictatorship. The first gas stations have run out of fuel, and those that still have it are hiking their prices dramatically. Fuel may be rationed for an extended period of time, and once this occurs, food will unavoidably follow.

According to one IT expert, the Colonial Pipeline from Houston (Texas) to Linden (New Jersey) could have been operational again in a matter of hours since damaged gear could have been swiftly replaced since most computer servers nowadays are Virtual Machines (VMs). If just the software had been damaged, the outage would have just been a few minutes long. As a result, the pipeline had many backups in every way.

Because no recovery was announced until the end of the week, this IT specialist believes that the gasoline shortages are being caused arbitrarily. Diesel is still used in trucks, but only for a limited time. When they come to a halt today or tomorrow, the stores will swiftly empty, threatening absolute fear and pandemonium.

After a week, the country will come to a halt, after two weeks, the drinking water supply will be jeopardized, and after four weeks, civilization will be finished.

North Carolina's governor has proclaimed a state of emergency and has temporarily (?) rationed petrol. The pumps of major businesses such as Shell and BP are now facing supply issues as well.

Is this a dress rehearsal for the recently anticipated major cyber-attack?

Unless the government repairs the pipeline within a few days, the already-started run on the final traces of gasoline will be followed by a run on the supermarkets. Indeed, it is highly conceivable that this 'false flag' was a practice run for the massive cyber-crisis previously foreshadowed by the WEF, which is to crush the whole West - including Europe - in order to crush the final remains of opposition to communist control of our country.

Of course, the Russians will be blamed for everything, which, as our readers well aware, is designed to rally the still-crazy masses behind the also-planned Third World War against Russia (and possibly China).

Complaining? Not if you voted in favor of this system.

Voters of the leftist and socialist parties, in particular, should not complain, because these parties, like almost

117

all left-wing opposition parties, openly support the Great Reset / Build Back Better / Agenda-21/2030 agenda and have been doing everything in their power for many years to make this future a reality for you and your (grand)children.

Except for themselves, of course, because, like in every communist and fascist dictatorships throughout history, the power elite will make certain that they are never impacted by their own rock-hard freedom and wealth-destroying laws.

Chapter 21: Food crisis

Europe has entered a comprehensive systemic crisis, with Germany already blaming 'cyber assaults' (of course, by 'the Russians,' which should prepare the populace for a massive conflict — 'The loss of 0.025 percent of the world's population does not warrant the ruin of the global economy.'

The 'Great Reset' of our secure and affluent society, purposefully started in motion by an airway virus, is going to be felt much more strongly. More and more signs point to Europe being on the verge of a food catastrophe with sky-high prices. Meanwhile, politicians and the media continue to pass on, rationalize, and sometimes even praise all of the blame for the suffering that has already occurred and is on its way.

The Food Price Index (FFPI) of the United Nations Food and Agriculture Organization (FAO) increased by 2.3 points (2.2 percent) in one month to 107.5 in December 2020, marking the seventh consecutive increase. The FFPI stood at 53.1 points in 2002, peaked at 131.9 points in 2011 as a result of the financial crisis, and then fell to slightly under 100.

Food, energy, and banking crises all at once

That governments exploit completely normal, natural, and harmless to the great majority of people biological alterations to prolong and/or enhance lockdown measures and limits on liberty, food supply lines will experience similar challenges as the electronics sector is presently experiencing (major shortage of microchips).

There are already fears in Germany that fruit and vegetable shortages are impending. They have also found a so-called cause: cyber attacks, which will, of course, be blamed on "the Russians." The horrible World Economic Forum of Klaus Schwab, the diabolical brain behind the 'Great Reset,' also anticipates cyber attacks on the power system and the financial sector.

Historical concept: blaming others for your own actions.

Basic food and energy are also getting increasingly pricey, and serious issues with bank accounts and internet payments should have you ready to commit to a massive conflict, most likely against Russia. In reality, energy disruptions will be created by a shift away from coal, oil, and gas, since a shift to unreliable and expensive wind, solar, and biomass is necessary. Furthermore, the next major banking crisis has been in the works for years, and it will be exploited to push through a fully digital payment system with a digital euro.

It's an old, known historical principle that's been utilized a lot: blame the party you consider the adversary for the issues you've created, and you'll have their support. Unfortunately, few people read history books now, or they refuse to learn from them ('this time we'll do it better,' 'this time things will be different') because they believe they are far brighter. (What is our opinion? Quite the contrary).

Or you have studied for it, and you have used the societal manipulating and undermining neo-Marxist strategies that authoritarian and dictatorial governments have used so many times before to your own people in an exceedingly sophisticated way, and let them be thankful for it as well.

'Did they have inside information, or is this a shady scheme?'

In this regard, American economist Martin Armstrong points to the well-known 'Event 201' pandemic simulation in October 2019, in which everything done from 2020 onwards was discussed, drafted, and worked out in detail in advance, complete with the deliberate sowing of fear and panic over a common coronavirus.

'Did they have foresight into the future, or is there a nefarious plot to lower population and CO_2, neatly creating global slaughter, as some now believe? Such conspiracy ideas often emerge when there are secret meetings and elite groups that believe they are exalted above the lower classes, which they see as the 'Great Scum.'

Conspiracy theories, on the other hand, are long gone, because all of these wicked schemes can be read, heard, and seen openly in the publications of major groups like the WEF. Although some of them, such as "In 2030 you will own nothing and be happy," were taken off after causing quite a sensation. That won't stop authoritarian bureaucrats from forcing this dreadful future on you and me (but not on themselves) in 2030. (but probably much earlier).

Food scarcity has caused widespread societal unrest (and possibly war)

In any event, food shortages and increasing costs are certain between now and 2024. 'This will cause significant social and political instability,' warns Armstrong. 'The EU government's mishandling might be their undoing. After all, as a result of such mismanagement, many people have lost their employment as a result of having to stay at home during the crisis, and their purchasing power has plummeted at the same time. This is the worst-case scenario, and it makes me wonder if these leaders are indeed that foolish, or simply that cunning.'

We believe both of them. Devious, because this systemic crisis has been planned to all intents and purposes, including fully controlling and directing the mainstream media, with the goal of creating a dictatorial EU superstate that will be (and already is) a technocratic mix of the former Soviet system and today's communist China.

Stupid, because they believe that their 'Great Reset / Build Back Better / Green New Deal' coup against free society will work in the long run, so that by 2030, the Bidens of our time will have fulfilled their hoped-for climatic utopia. Evidently, these individuals have lost their sense of reality, since otherwise, they should realize that with an all-or-nothing approach, nothing of our civilization would survive by 2030 at the latest.

In any event, Armstrong believes that the world is unprepared for a food crisis, which will surely be triggered by the continuation of the current measures. Shortages will be more severe in major cities. The high VAT and taxes in Europe will be the final nail in the coffin for many. Then supermarkets do not need to be supplied for only a few days for widespread panic, anarchy, and violence to erupt.

According to the economist, stock market speculators will be punished, but we believe a political offender, most likely Russian President Vladimir Putin, will also be implicated. If that is the case, it is convenient if you have already sparked a large regional conflict in, say, Ukraine, and maybe the Middle East, before then. After all, we've seen how easily supply networks can be disrupted by a single container ship (Suez Canal).

Bill Gates is one of the most significant contributors to this catastrophe.

Armstrong then offers another 'conspiracy theory,' according to which Bill Gates is now the largest owner of farmland in the United States. True or not, it has been proved that he has 'purchased' the WHO and has it in his pocket, as well as the American CDC and, probably, all equivalent agencies in Europe. Furthermore, he has stock in every major pharmaceutical business and is the main force behind the GAVI vaccination partnership. So, though Gates will undoubtedly be one of the most significant contributors to the years-long catastrophe, the Western media, which he co-controls, will never be permitted to publish that.

Hundreds of thousands of farms have vanished in both America and Europe over the last decade, mostly due to ever-increasing taxes and ever-stricter 'environment' rules and legislation. Governments were able to acquire enormous tracts of land at extremely low costs for projects like as housing, "sustainable" energy, and "nature restoration." This long-standing anti-farming strategy threatens to amplify the looming food catastrophe.

The loss of 0.025 percent of the world's population does not warrant the ruin of the global economy.

124

'Meanwhile, there is a rush to immunize everyone against a disease that is no more fatal than the flu,' Armstrong added. 'The number of Covid fatalities is so overblown that our politicians are either the stupidest or the most deceitful persons on the planet. During the Spanish flu, 50 million people died, accounting for 3.125 percent of the world's population at the time (1.6 billion). There are now 7.8 billion people on the planet, and 2 million deceased individuals account for only 0.02564 percent of that. This in no way excuses the collapse of the global economy.'

The Nuremberg Agreements have been ignored and even reversed.

'The mainstream media shamelessly applauds the lockdowns and terrorizes the population.' It is becoming clear that immunizations protect no one from catching Covid and may even put them in greater danger if the population is wiped out by one of the new mutations. Meanwhile, pharmaceutical firms are completely insulated from responsibility. All international leaders agreed at Nuremberg to prohibit such medical experiments on the general people if they had not yet (or not properly) been tested on animals. The vaccinations that are being administered have not even been tested on rats or mice.'

(This is due, in part, to far-left, Marxist 'woke' thinking, which has stripped people of any higher spirituality and regards them as nothing more than a biological machine incapable of transcending animal life. Indeed, by utilizing humans as guinea pigs rather than animals, people are positioned under animals. It goes without saying that this heinous anti-human mindset paves the way for a bloodbath, a genocide, the likes of which the world has never seen before and will most likely never see again (since there will be far too few of us remaining).

Chapter 22: The next world war?

The Russian reaction to the provocations of US bombers was unprecedented: three nuclear submarines burst through the polar ice at the same time. The United States could be annihilated in minutes from that vantage point.

The tremendously concerning situation in Ukraine is now reaching the (alternative) media. Analyst Tom Luongo now claims that the West, led by Joe Biden, is preparing for a confrontation with Russia in Ukraine, maybe as soon as after the Orthodox Passover (May 2). The fundamental reason is because the Kremlin refuses to sign on to the World Economic Forum's, United Nations', and European Union's Great Reset 2030 climate plan. Western politicians have gone wild to the point that they are making the fatal mistake of assuming that President Putin will not dare to defend his nation to the death against this worldwide coup. In doing so, Washington, Brussels, and The Hague are deliberately putting themselves at danger of a large-scale nuclear battle erupting.

Now, the long-desired conflict against Russia threatens to put a stop to the European fantasy of a "climate paradise" in 2030, which would, in any event, finish years early in a dreadful nightmare full of communist poverty and technocratic oppression for 99 percent of the people.

Who is the true "soulless killer"?

Biden had only been president for a few months when he referred to Putin as a "killer without a soul." The Russian president answered with "it takes one to know one," in his usual calm and masterful manner, and then invited Biden to a direct discussion.

Of course, Biden declined, because the demented Biden, who frequently forgets where he is and who he is speaking to during speeches (there is now footage showing him with cards in his hand with "who is who" pictures on them, as well as a complete script that he has to follow), is clearly no match for the Russian leader. The Democrats are well aware of this, which is why they want to keep him away from the press as much as possible.

'And then there was that humiliating press conference the other day.' Is he running for re-election in 2024? He won't even be alive at that point. But, hey, he didn't run in 2020 either, so what's the difference?" scoffs Luongo.

Russian retaliation to American provocations

In any event, relations between the two superpowers have been 'appalling' since the nomination of phony President Biden in a flashy political coup. Americans are doing nothing to change this, in fact, exactly the contrary. Recently, Biden dispatched strategic B-52 bombers to launch a fake strike on Russia across the

North Pole. The jets returned to Canada, but a response from the Kremlin was unavoidable. Three Russian nuclear submarines (a one-time occurrence) broke through the polar ice at the same time. From that vantage point, the United States could be completely annihilated in fifteen minutes.

Obama says Ukraine is 'Biden's project.'

Ukraine is 'Biden's project,' declared Barack Obama. The Bidens are embroiled in corruption in Ukraine, as we have widely exposed in recent years.

According to Luongo, the situation in Ukraine is "far more hazardous" than we are told. We've previously given you one possible explanation, and it's not very reassuring: the Western elite may try to overwhelm the populace with a sudden conflict, falsely presenting it as a "Russian surprise strike," to which "of course, we must reply promptly." You may not be allowed time to examine what is actually going on, which is that this conflict is only supporting the interests of the 'Great Reset' climate elite, who must be pushed through at the expense of the general public.

The escalating war in Ukraine is "all of this and more." The initiative to admit Ukraine to NATO and the EU has long been a goal of neocons such as Victoria Nuland and neoliberals such as Joe Biden. It is a key component of the World Economic Forum's ambition to encircle

Russia, obstructing the goal of Eurasian integration that may serve as a bulwark against their 'brave new world.'

The West wishes to compel Russia and China to conform to the Great Reset.

Biden has invited Putin and Chinese President Xi Jinping to a climate meeting in April, the agenda of which will be dictated by the World Economic Forum. Because both Putin and Xi have stated that they would not engage in the Great Reset and Agenda 2030, as well as Klaus Schwab's "Fourth Industrial Revolution" (in actuality, the Great Industrial Deconstruction), this meeting is bound to fail from the start (though no doubt some lip service will be paid, but after that Russia and China will just go their separate ways).

'This summit appears to be a massive waste of time, because everyone across the globe will be threatened with what they can anticipate from the West in terms of policy - until someone finally puts these lunatic individuals out of their misery,' Luongo said. 'For example, the United Kingdom under dictator Boris Johnson is falling more and further into a full totalitarian nightmare as a result of Covid-19, while anti-Russian propaganda is reaching record heights.'

War in the Donbass, potentially as soon as tomorrow

Ukraine is "directly implicated in all of this crap about climate change." Putin also believes that Biden will not allow any escalation in Ukraine because he is tethered to it and must complete the work he began in 2014 with the toppling of (the democratically elected president) Viktor Yanukovich. As a result, we will witness something far worse than Victoria Nuland's "cookie campaign" for liberty. We shall have a fight over the Donbass shortly, most likely shortly after Orthodox Easter and the melting of the winter.'

According to Luongo, Putin has made tremendous efforts to halt this fatal downward cycle, 'because he understands where this leads.' It will be a showdown in which Putin will have to either watch Ukraine launch a war against the Russian-speaking people in the Donbass and Crimea with Western support, or interfere anyhow, knowing that the West would instantly use this to paint him as the 'aggressor.'

The West is preparing for an escalation; the EU has refused dialogue for years.

The West, according to Luongo, has no choice but to escalate since it stands to gain nothing from a return to quiet, peace, and collaboration. 'Russia must be subdued or destroyed for the Great Reset to work and Europe to remain an important global actor.' That entails control of the Black Sea and the conquest of Crimea.'

Russian Foreign Minister Sergei Lavrov recently voiced worry that the EU has not maintained diplomatic connections with the Kremlin after the 2014 vote, in which the people of Crimea declared nearly overwhelmingly that they wanted to belong to the Russian homeland. 'Diplomacy between big nations has all but vanished.' Biden's plain reluctance to engage in open dialogue with Putin is a major concern.'

The Great Reset is hampered by Eurasian dominance over oil and gas.

Everything since the 'corona' of totalitarian and oppressive measures in the West, including the gradual destruction of SMEs and freedom, is in line with the WEF's 'Great Reset,' which includes the total destruction of the 'fossil' economy and, with it, the end of energy security and affordability for Western citizens.

However, if the production of oil, gas, and coal continues under Eurasian control, the Atlanteans' megalomaniacal ambitions will never come true. There isn't much time left for them to impose their worldwide communist climate-vaccine tyranny, since Western public opposition to the entire devastation of their society and future grows by the day.

The West will not have a joyful finish to the war.

'If there is a conflict in the Donbass this spring, it will not have a nice conclusion in which America (and Europe) will continue in power in the future, but it will be the moment when we understand that our descent into irrelevance has hastened.'

With a bit of bad luck, this deterioration may even result in a nuclear battle, in which Russia (perhaps aided by China) decides to chop off the 'head of the serpent' that has been an ever-increasing threat to humanity's existence for so long. This may include a (limited) nuclear strike on cities like Washington, New York, London, Brussels, and Rome (the Vatican), as well as Los Angeles (Hollywood), Paris, Strasbourg, Berlin, Frankfurt, and The Hague.

We can be certain of one thing: if it were up to Vladimir Putin, it would never have come to that. It remains to be seen if there will be enough time for the fear, hunger for power, and sheer lunacy that have utterly overtaken the cities named to give way to a restoration of reason, sobriety, and, most importantly, true concern for the well and future of all residents. Unfortunately, the omens for this are now pointing in the other direction.

If China joins in, WW3 is a fact!

If China becomes embroiled in a major battle with the West, such as a war with Taiwan, Japan and Australia might be targeted, and hostilities might erupt between North and South Korea, India and Pakistan, India and China, Iran and Saudi Arabia, and Iran and Israel. Then World War III will become a reality.

For the time being, we are anticipating that the final major global conflagration will not occur until somewhere between 2025 and 2030. Nonetheless, everyone will see that a conflict in Ukraine might easily tumble all the other dominoes far sooner.

Chapter 23: Pressure from the east?

How would America respond to Chinese military support for a declaring Puerto Rico independent?

A spokesman for China's Ministry of Defense has demanded in an official statement that the United States cut "all military ties with Taiwan. America has been Taiwan's largest arms supplier for years. Beijing still considers the island a renegade province that should be rejoined with China no matter what. If the U.S. stands in the way of this, "it means war.

'The complete reunification of China is a historical necessity, and the great rejuvenation of the Chinese nation is an unstoppable trend,' declared Ren Guoqiang (photo). 'The people's common aspirations are peace and stability across the Taiwan Strait. An 'independent Taiwan' is a dead end, and an attempt to do so means war.'

The Chinese are demanding that the government in Washington return to uncompromising support for the one-China policy. Shortly after President Biden took office, U.S. officials spoke openly for the first time about an "independent Taiwan," which was very much against Beijing's wishes.

On June 15, as many as 28 Chinese Air Force aircraft, including bombers capable of carrying nuclear weapons, penetrated Taiwan's air defense zone. This was by no means the first time this had happened, but by such a large number.

Yesterday, Taiwan's foreign minister, Joseph Wu, warned that the country should "prepare" for a possible Chinese invasion. 'We cannot take a risk... Now that the Chinese government says they do not reject the use of force, and are conducting military exercises around Taiwan, then we are more likely to believe that this is real.'

How would America react to Chinese support for an independent Puerto Rico?

From the Chinese point of view, the situation is more or less comparable to a fictitious declaration of independence by the Caribbean island of Puerto Rico, which was taken by the U.S. in 1898. The federal government in Washington then does not recognize this independence, whereupon China begins arming the island.

How would the regime in Washington respond? Given U.S. history, presumably with brute force much sooner than the Chinese could do with Taiwan now.

Nevertheless, we believe that all peoples should have the right to self-determination, i.e. to real democracy. Not leaders, governments and institutions, but citizens should have the last word. However, this is hardly the case anywhere, certainly not in the West, where democracy has been completely dismantled and is only a sham for an increasingly authoritarian technocracy.

Chapter 24: Berlin is a military target

"In 4 weeks, a World War might be unleashed in Ukraine as Putin sends 4,000 troops and tanks to the border," The Sun, Britain's most famous tabloid newspaper, recently headlined.

Whether it causes a stir or not, the announcement that China would soon send 5,000 troops to Iran is extremely dangerous. Furthermore, Tehran demonstrated a cruise missile capable of hitting Berlin, and the mullahs guaranteed their support for Russia in the event that Ukraine launched a frontal attack on Crimea and the Donbass, sparking a NATO-led war.

Only a "psychoanalyst" can understand Moscow's aims, according to Russian military analyst Pavel Felgenhauer, who also warned that developments might lead to a catastrophic war within a month.

All the sorrow brought upon by the coup in 2014

In 2014, the CIA orchestrated a violent coup in Ukraine with the help of the US and EU. The country's democratically elected president was toppled and replaced with a Western-backed puppet dictatorship, which launched a murderous war against the country's Russian-speaking populace in the east.

In order to bring Ukraine into NATO as quickly as possible, a highly probable "false flag" attack was carried out on a passenger plane (MH17) flying from Amsterdam to Malaysia, which was deliberately directed by Ukrainian air traffic control over war zones.

Russia's major naval port in Sevastopol (Crimea) would be lost, and once NATO bases are erected in Ukraine, Russia's nuclear weapons could be destroyed by American missiles in a surprise attack in minutes, putting the country defenseless.

China dispatches 5000 troops to Iran, which has launched a missile capable of striking Berlin.

However, an axis is forming that is fed up with years of American-led Western racism and war-mongering, as well as all those ostensibly "peace and democracy" missions that have murdered millions of people just this century. The Islamic Republic of Iran, for example, unveiled a new cruise missile with a range of 3,000 kilometers capable of hitting Berlin last Saturday.

Meanwhile, China has announced significant billion-dollar expenditures in Iran, including the deployment of 5,000 troops and the establishment of new military outposts.

Is the West's already-disappeared light going out for good?

In January 2018, the BBC in the United Kingdom aired a simulated news program about the start of a war between NATO and Russia, with nuclear weapons being launched after only one hour. A similar fictitious announcement of World War III with Russia was broadcast by the German public broadcaster.

Call it scaremongering or predictive programming, but one thing is clear at the start of 2021: in recent years, we have only had leaders, media, and institutions in the West, as well as in our own country, who can only lie and cheat coldly about important issues, whether it is about Russia, the coronavirus, vaccinations, or the climate. The light, like their leaders, has long since vanished for those who fall for this with their eyes open and/or sometimes even think it's a good thing. Worse, what was previously light has been renamed darkness, and what was darkness has been renamed light.

Russia, China, and Iran are all under fire, but it's unclear how much time the West has left to come to its senses, look in the mirror, and admit how far we've fallen as a so-called advanced 'civilization.' If we keep going at our current rate, it won't be more than 10 years or so, and if The Sun is correct for once, it won't be more than 10 weeks. When this more likely catastrophe occurs, it will be unexpected for the vast majority of us, and totally our own responsibility, in our opinion.

Chapter 25: The West against Russia

'Extremely serious threat to national security' is only one step away from declaring war.

Because of the "unique and unprecedented threat that Russia represents to the national security, foreign policy, and economics of the United States," US President Joe Biden has proclaimed a "state of national emergency." The United States is expelling ten Russian diplomats and implementing new restrictions. Russia is intensively preparing its army and fleet for a great (global) conflict, which it worries - and rightfully so - that the increasingly aggressive Americans are out to start.

The only people who stood in the way of the Western globalists' "Great Reset" were Trump and Putin. Trump was exonerated thanks to the largest election fraud in history; now it's Russia's turn. America's and Europe's mad neo-Marxist technocrats seemed to believe they can win a war against Russia without causing too much damage.

Russia is preparing for war.

As a result, Russia will expel a large number of American diplomats. The Kerch Strait, which connects the Crimean peninsula and the Russian mainland, will be closed to all navy and foreign-owned boats starting next week.

The closure will last until October, and mainly affects the Ukrainian port cities of Mariupol and Berdyansk.

Near the Ukrainian border, Russian armored vehicles and trucks were spotted with so-called "invasion stripes." Clear white stripes are painted on the vehicles to protect them from being shot down by their own planes and tanks. This appears to signal that Russia is really considering putting an end to the Western-backed Neo-Nazi administration in Kiev, which, as our readers are aware, has been attempting for years to create a massive NATO-Russia war.

Ukraine claims that more than 110,000 Russian troops, 330 airplanes, and 240 helicopters will be stationed along its border. Kiev alleges that Russia is transferring nuclear weapons to Crimea, but we have our doubts. Indeed, Russia is under no obligation to do so; Ukraine could theoretically be annihilated by nuclear weapons launched from anywhere on the planet.

The majority of the Russian Pacific Fleet has returned to Vladivostok and is being properly resupplied there, according to satellite pictures. At least one naval warship is receiving "new" missiles on board. This suggests that Russia expects any conflict to go beyond Ukraine and into the rest of the world.

It appears that a military clash between the US and Russia is only a matter of time.

142

Now that the US president has branded Russia a "danger to national security," and Biden has given the command to respond to that "threat," the military clash that Washington and Brussels have long desired appears to be only a matter of time, potentially just a few weeks away.

President Putin has long recognized how the West operates and, as a result, has turned down the offer of a meeting with Vice President Joe Biden. This would be nothing more than the world-famous Western blackmail diplomacy ('we want peace, but only on our terms, and if you don't agree, our bombs and missiles will follow'), which has claimed the lives of millions of people in the last two decades alone.

'The war-mongering neocons are doing exactly what they had to stop doing in 2016 when Trump's victory shattered their satanic preparations for war with Russia... Then there were many who claimed Trump was dangerous,' says Hall Turner, an American radio presenter. 'This senile demented half-wit is going to be the ruin of us all,' says Biden.

We presumably don't need to explain what this says about the mental state of European leaders, who were so shocked when this warmongering 'half-wit' managed to wrestle the Trump they despised out of the White House, nor do they appear to care what happens to you, me, and hundreds of millions of other people.

Chapter 26: The new "Green Deal"

Ocasio-'Green Cortez's New Deal' entails 'the extinction of all life on Earth' - 'If fossil fuels are abolished, every tree on the planet will be chopped down.'

Dr. Patrick Moore, co-founder of Greenpeace, has slammed Alexandria Ocasio-Cortez (picture), the new darling of America's 'progressive' left. The 'Democratic Socialist' has proposed a 'Green New Deal,' which would cost tens of billions of dollars and, according to many detractors, will return the United States to pre-industrial civilization. Moore called Ocasio-Cortez a "hypocrite" and a "pompous dork" because executing her demand to phase out fossil fuels—which the European administration has already begun to do with the natural gas shutdown—will result in "mass fatalities."

Moore quit "his" Greenpeace years ago when the environmental organization was hijacked from within by far-left anarchists like Ocasio-Cortez.

All flights and automobiles must be grounded (except for her own)

The "Green New Deal" proposes that the United States abandon all reliance on oil, gas, and nuclear power. Trains must replace air transport (even across seas), and 99 percent of all automobiles must be phased out.

Of course, with the exception of the governing class, things went on as normal. According to the New York Post, Ocasio has a massive "carbon footprint," in part because her campaign staff relies nearly entirely on normal gasoline automobiles. She flew 66 times between May 2017 and December of last year, compared to only 18 times by rail, which, if she had her way, everyone would be obliged to convert to.

Socialist funds continue to push for free housing.

Furthermore, every structure in the United States will have to be extensively changed or possibly rebuilt to fulfill extremely stringent climatic regulations. Cortez proposes funding for millions of government positions for this reason. Those who do not wish to work will, by the way, be free to stay at home and will no longer be required to pay housing costs. But who would desire that?

How does "AOC" intend to fund its green utopia? Simply put, the only way to pay its draconian and enormously expensive plans is to turn on the money presses. Because 'we are going to get it right this time,' Cortez stated in an earlier interview, the fact that this socialism has resulted in widespread poverty and misery throughout history should not be a concern.

'This plan entails the annihilation of all life.' Brilliant'

According to the Green New Deal, all greenhouse emissions must be eliminated from the environment. Moore's response: 'Technically (scientifically) speaking, this implies deleting all water vapor and all CO2, which implies eradicating all life.' Brilliant.'

'If you don't like the deal, you should just come up with your own bold proposal to tackle the global climate catastrophe,' AOC tweeted later. Until then, we're in command, and you're simply yelling from the stands.'

The depletion of fossil fuels will result in mass deaths.'

Moore retorted, 'pompous dork.' You have no strategy to feed 8 billion people without using fossil fuels, or to deliver food into cities. Horses? If fossil fuels are outlawed, every tree on the planet will be felled in order to provide fuel for cooking and heating. You will kill a lot of people... You are nothing more than a hypocrite like the rest of them, with ZERO competence in any field you claim to be knowledgeable in.'

'You are suffering from illusions if you think fossil fuels will disappear anytime soon,' Moore added later in response to a tweet from another climate zealot who said that 'the end of fossil fuels is certain.' Perhaps in 500 years. The attitude of AOC is reckless and insulting. She is a newbie who pretends to be intelligent. If her sort is in command, she will wreck us.'

Our other books

Check out our other books for other unreported news, exposed facts and debunked truths, and more.

Join the exclusive Rebel Press Media Circle!

You will get new updates about the unreported reality delivered in your inbox every Friday.

Sign up here today:

https://campsite.bio/rebelpressmedia